CASE STUDIES
FOR THE FIRST YEAR

AN ODYSSEY INTO
CRITICAL THINKING
AND PROBLEM SOLVING

Robert M. Sherfield

Rhonda J. Montgomery

Patricia G. Moody

PEARSON
Prentice
Hall

Upper Saddle River, New Jersey
Columbus, Ohio

Library of Congress Cataloging-in-Publication Data

Sherfield, Robert M.
    Case studies for the first year : an odyssey into critical thinking
and problem solving / Robert M. Sherfield, Rhonda J. Montgomery,
Patricia G. Moody.
       p.   cm.
Includes bibliographical references.
    ISBN 0-13-111525-1
    1. Critical thinking--Study and teaching (Higher)--Case studies. 2.
Case method--Study and teaching (Higher) I. Montgomery, Rhonda J. II.
Moody, Patricia G. III. Title.

LB2395.35 .S54 2004
378.1'79--dc21
                                        2003045991

Vice President and Publisher: Jeffery W. Johnston
Senior Acquisitions Editor: Sande Johnson
Assistant Editor: Cecilia Johnson
Editorial Assistant: Erin Anderson
Production Editor: Holcomb Hathaway
Design Coordinator: Diane C. Lorenzo
Cover Designer: Thomas Borah
Cover Photo: Getty One
Production Manager: Pamela D. Bennett
Director of Marketing: Ann Castel Davis
Marketing Manager: Christina Quadhamer
Compositor: Aerocraft Charter Art Service
Printer/Binder: R. R. Donnelley & Sons Company
Cover Printer: The Lehigh Press, Inc.

Dedication

FOR ROBB:
Tina Eliopulos

FOR RHONDA:
*Mick and Jackie
Montgomery*

FOR PAT:
*Jackson, Lauren,
and Josh Moody*

Pearson Education Ltd.
Pearson Education Australia Pty. Limited
Pearson Education Singapore Pte. Ltd.
Pearson Education North Asia Ltd.
Pearson Education Canada, Ltd.
Pearson Educación de Mexico, S.A. de C.V.
Pearson Education–Japan
Pearson Education Malaysia Pte. Ltd.

15

ISBN 0-13-111525-1

Contents

Acknowledgments

We would like to thank the following individuals for their support and assistance with this project: Dr. Ron Remington, President, Community College of Southern Nevada; Dr. Robert Palinchak, Vice President, Community College of Southern Nevada; Dr. Don Smith, Dean, Community College of Southern Nevada; Dr. Charles Mosely, Department Chair, Community College of Southern Nevada; Dr. Carol Harter, President, University of Nevada, Las Vegas; Dr. Stuart Mann, Dean, University of Nevada, Las Vegas; Professor Patti Shock, Department Chair, University of Nevada, Las Vegas; Dr. Andrew A. Sorensen, President, University of South Carolina; and Dr. Jerome Odom, Provost, University of South Carolina.

In addition, we would like to thank the following reviewers for their constructive feedback regarding the manuscript: Chris Caplinger, Georgia Southern University; Connie Engelman, Nassau Community College; Judith Lynch, Kansas State University; Howard Y. Masuda, California State University, Los Angeles; and Jon M. Young, Fayetteville State University.

Finally, a very special thank you to these individuals at Prentice Hall, for the tireless work with and support of our many projects: Robin Baliszewski, Jeff Johnston, Christina Quadhamer, and Cecilia Johnson. And to Sande Johnson, our editor, who is also our mentor, our advisor, our guide, and our friend—we thank you sincerely for all that you do and all that you are.

Introduction to Case Studies

Home So Soon?

THE CASE OF HARRIETT AND BELINDA

Harriett walks into the apartment to find Belinda asleep on the sofa. There are pizza boxes on the floor, soda cans all over, and cigarette butts spilled on the side tables. The house reeks of smoke and beer. "How can she be such a pig?" Harriett thinks to herself. "I was only gone one night." She walks over to her desk to put her book bag down only to discover that someone has turned an entire can of beer over on her new Biology textbook. "That's it!" she yells. "BELINDA!"

Belinda does not move. Harriett walks over to the sofa and shakes her. "What happened here last night?" Harriett asks in a stern voice.

"Huh," moans Belinda in a voice fraught with sleep and alcohol.

"Oh, you're home already," Belinda moans.

"Yeah, I'm home, and someone ruined my $110.00 Biology book. What did you do here last night? I thought you were going to the study group."

"Well, the study group came over here, and we ordered some pizza," Belinda says.

"And beer . . . and cigarettes . . . and . . ."

"Chill out, girl! This isn't nuclear war," Belinda says sharply.

"Chill out? Look at this place. You don't have any respect for me or where we live. This is my home too," Harriett exclaims.

"I'll clean it up tonight," Belinda says. "I've gotta get some sleep and go to class later."

"Tonight? Tonight? What am I supposed to do all day? Sit around here and study in this filthy mess?" Harriett replies.

"You want a place to study?" Belinda asks as she takes her arm and slides pizza boxes, cans, and ashes onto the floor from the coffee table. "There you go girl . . . study!"

Belinda turns her face toward the back of the sofa and pulls the covers over her head.

- How would you feel if you were Harriett?
- How would you feel if you were Belinda?
- Shouldn't Belinda be able to have friends over to study?
- Did Harriett overreact?
- Was Belinda rude and insensitive?
- Should Belinda replace the Biology book?
- What are the solutions to this problem?
- Have you ever been involved in a similar situation at home?
- What are the consequences of your solution(s)?
- Where can Belinda and Harriett go for help?

WHAT IS A CASE STUDY?

The case study method was developed at Harvard University in the 1800s as a way to teach medicine, business, and law. Simply stated, a case study is a story. Cases ask us to look inside the lives, actions, challenges, and trials of ordinary people in extraordinary situations. You are usually given a scenario with details about real-life situations and are left to decipher what happened, what is the major problem, who did what, who or what caused the problem(s) associated with the case, and what needs to be done. Cases are intentionally written without endings. Your job in the case analysis is to bring the scenario to a logical closing. Note that there are *no* right or wrong answers in case studies. Granted, some answers will be more appropriate, more logical, better thought out, and more applicable than others, but no reasonable suggestions will be wrong.

Usually built on real-life incidents, cases can be long, highly structured, and extremely detailed, or they can be painfully short and intentionally vague. Harriett and Belinda's case is not a long one, but cases can be even shorter. An example of a short case study follows:

> You are taking Human Anatomy, and your professor has made several derogatory remarks about women majoring in the sciences. He always selects males to participate in classroom discussions, and he frequently uses the phrase, "men and girls," not "men and women" or "boys and girls."

While this brief case is vague and gives few details, it can lead to much discussion on sexual inequity, sexual harassment, sexual bias, accessibility to classes, discrimination, diversity, open-mindedness, fairness, comfort levels, male verses female roles in society, career options, campus politics, and the professor's approachability.

This short case could lead to a discussion that lasts the entire class period or, if assigned, could lead to a lengthy paper on one of the above topics. While this case was lacking in detail, even the lengthiest cases may not give you every detail associated with the incident. The beauty of working with and learning through cases is that you have the opportunity to make educated assumptions, learn problem solving and critical thinking skills, and engage with your peers in discussions or debates over important issues.

WHY CASE STUDIES AND WHY THIS BOOK?

We have used the term *Odyssey* in our subtitle because an odyssey is an intellectual or spiritual quest. It is a journey that takes you places you have never been. The word *odyssey* is derived from the Greek name *Odusseus*, the king of Ithaca, who wandered for 10 years after the Trojan War and the fall of Troy. We want this book to be a journey for you—a journey that will open your mind to new possibilities, unseen solutions, and uncharted actions.

The use of cases among peers can motivate you to get more involved with the class and in the discussions or debates. Properly used, cases engage every student in effective involvement and learning and promote critical thinking and problem solving skills. Case studies encourage cooperative learning and teach the value of teamwork. They compel you to strengthen your listening and communication abilities. They ask you to explore your own value system and your cultural/social morals. They take you beyond the classroom experience by asking you to discover the implications of the issues for society. Cases ask you to look beyond the immediate to see the bigger picture. Finally, they can bring about personal change and promote internal growth.

In this book, you will encounter 42 case studies derived from real-life incidents at colleges and businesses across the nation. We have interviewed students, professors, and leaders to capture many situations that actually happen in the lives of college students. In some cases, we have written stories that parallel incidents reported in newspapers and on television. In short, the cases you will read in this book are situations that many of your peers face on a daily basis. We hope that your active participation in—and honest, straightforward discussions of—these case studies will not only help your peers but also add to the quality of your education and life.

DECONSTRUCTING THE MYTHS OF CASE STUDIES

Most students have been exposed to case studies on some level over the years. If your professors have properly used the case study approach, you already understand that cases are not easy and that it takes determination and much critical thought to fully understand and decode the case in order to make recommendations. However, several myths still exist about cases that need to be debunked. Understanding these myths can help you use case studies more effectively.

MYTH #1: Case studies are easy, and I don't have to do that much. Wrong! Cases may be easy to read, but cases often are filled with details, dates, numbers, names, places, and multiple situations. To fully participate in the case, you need to do more than show up.

MYTH #2: Case studies do not take much time at all. It is true that some cases are extremely short and may seem to have a clear-cut ending, but as described previously in the brief case presented, you could spend hours on the smallest details of the case.

MYTH #3: Everybody loves case studies. Many professors wish this were the case, but in truth, some students do not like case studies because they force everyone to participate. You can't sit in the back of the room with a closed mouth and a closed mind. Because cases demand involvement from everyone, some students see them as threatening.

MYTH #4: The case itself gives you all you need to know. Most of the time this is *not* true. As previously stated, cases can be vague and the writer may intentionally leave out details to instigate more discussion. Cases are one of the few places where logical, educated guesses and assumptions are encouraged and often needed. You also may have to research some of the issues if you are not familiar with them, in order to fully and actively participate.

MYTH #5: My opinion is all I need to work with a case study. Incorrect. While opinions are valued in case studies, you will need to draw on your keen listening skills, your critical thinking abilities, your reasoning and cleverness, your teamwork savvy, and your best communication proficiency. These are the elements that will help you discuss and learn from the case.

MYTH #6: All cases can be solved. Because real-life case studies deal with real life, human emotions and feelings, some cases may never be solved. Human nature is quirky and unpredictable, so cases built on real-life instances will be the same. At times you will simply have to agree to disagree and learn to accept the inevitability of finding no conclusion. Such is life. However, cases do ask for logical, reasonable, and critical thought.

MYTH #7: We will find the right answer. Cases often have numerous dimensions and underlying points that make them complex. Thus, it may be impossible to find an answer that is considered "right." You and your group may find an appropriate answer, but "right" is subjective and elusive at best. Caution: While there may be no "right" or "wrong" answers, your biggest challenge may be to determine which solution is "best" or "suitable" for the people involved. At times, this can be harder to determine than what is "right" or "wrong."

THE MYSTERY OF "X"—WHAT IS UNSPOKEN

The complexity and depth of a case study depend on the writer. We know that cases do not have endings, but we also must face the notion that not all cases tell the entire story. The writer may intentionally or unintentionally leave out details that cause you to estimate, guesstimate, assume, presume, and judge. This is one of the beauties, as well as one of the curses, of case studies. It is human nature to want the "whole story." However, if you have the entire story with a tidy ending, you have little left to learn from the incident. Cases are intended to help you learn how to think more critically and use your problem solving skills.

An old Native American saying states: "If you are my friend, you will hear what I am not saying." Cases exist along these lines. To be a successful detective, you have to listen for what is not said, read what is not written, see what is not visible, and feel what is not touchable. At the end of each case, you will be asked to analyze the situation. One of the questions asked of you will be, "What are some *logical assumptions* you can make about the case?"

The word *logical* means reasonable, valid, and clear. The word *assumption* means without proof or evidence. These two words seem to be juxtaposed. However, a *logical assumption* simply means that you are making a statement that has no proof but that is reasonable enough based on the facts given, the previous behaviors of individuals involved, the circumstances outlined, and the support of members of your group. Just because you and your group have made a logical assumption does not mean that it is true or that other individuals or groups will agree with your assessment.

CRITICAL THINKING AND CASE STUDIES

What do critical thinking and case studies have in common? Almost everything. It would be hard to evaluate a case study without a basic understanding of what critical thinking really is and how to apply the concepts of critical thinking to a case study.

There are almost as many definitions of critical thinking as there are people who try to define it. According to the *American Heritage Dictionary,* the word *critical* is defined as "careful and exact evaluation and judgment." *Thinking* is defined as "to reason about or reflect on; to ponder." *Critical thinking,* then, might be defined as evaluating and judging your reasoning and reflections. However, this definition is not a complete description. Critical thinking can also mean thinking deeper, being skeptical, questioning strongly held beliefs, or taking no information or opinion for granted. Note that critical thinking is not innate; it is a learned skill that every student can acquire and polish.

For this text, we will use the working definition of critical thinking as defined by Diane Helpern in her book *Thought and Knowledge: An Introduction to Critical Thinking* (1996). Helpern defines critical thinking as "thinking that is purposeful, reasoned, and goal directed—the kind of thinking involved in solving problems, formulating inferences, calculating livelihoods, and making decisions."

Critical thinking, then, is more than just having a thought or "casual" thinking. It is voluntarily and objectively evaluating and judging your thoughts. It is the ability to evaluate and judge the accuracy of information and the source of that information. It is a skill that you can learn through practice, trial and error, reflection, comparison, brainstorming, questioning, and research. It is a skill that will assist you in making logical decisions and inferences about your case studies.

THE IMPORTANCE OF CRITICAL THINKING

Critical thinking can serve you in many areas as a student and as a citizen in society. As a student, critical thinking can help you focus on issues, gather relevant and accurate information, remember facts, organize thoughts logically, analyze questions and problems, and manage your priorities. It can assist in your problem solving skills and help you control your emotions so that you can make rational judgments. It can help you produce new knowledge through research and analysis and help you determine the factual accuracy of printed and spoken words. It can help you detect bias and determine the relevance of arguments and persuasion.

As a citizen, critical thinking can help you get along with others. It can help you realize cause and effect in the world. It can assist you in financial planning, stress reduction, and health issues, and it can help you make rational, informed decisions in a variety of cultural and civic duties, such as voting, volunteering, or contributing money. Critical thinking is a skill valuable not only in the academic arena but also in relationships, neighborhood planning, environmental concerns, and lifelong goal setting, to name a few. It can help you and your family solve problems together. It can help you make decisions that permanently affect the lives of your family members, and it can help you choose the alternatives that are best for you, your family, and your friends.

In recent surveys, employers cited several qualities related to critical thinking as being crucial for success in the 21st-century workplace: problem solving skills, intellectual and idea-generating skills, and teamwork skills.

When working with your cases, critical thinking can assist you in looking at every side of the issue before making a judgment. It can help you find the details that noncritical thinkers would not seek. It can help you ask questions that will encourage rational discussion of the case incident.

A Six-Point Plan for Critical Thinking

As you begin to build and expand your critical thinking skills, consider the following six strategies for critical thinking:

Emotional restraint. Emotions play a vital role in our lives. They enable us to feel compassion, help others, reach out in times of need, and relate to others. However, emotions can cause some problems in your critical thinking process. You *do not* have to eliminate emotions from your thoughts, but it is crucial that you recognize when your emotions are clouding an issue.

Once a thought has been produced or introduced, many times we immediately form an opinion or judgment based on how our emotions make us *feel,* not on actual thought, evaluation, or analysis. Critical thinking requires us to pay special attention to emotions and attitudes so that we might get at the heart of the matter. Emotions such as anger, love, hatred, and fear can cloud our judgment and evaluation, causing us to make decisions that are not based on solid thinking. These emotions can cause us to ignore the truth.

Research. One of the most important aspects of becoming an educated citizen is the ability to learn how to learn. You must know how to seek and find answers to questions, reference bibliographical information, collect historical data, explore government documents, investigate advances in technology, and survey trends in society. Many students run to the library or log on to the Internet and take the first pieces of information that pop up. They do not know how to begin their research or how to distinguish scholarly research from writing in the popular press. As you begin to research your cases, keep these basic steps in mind:

- Have at least three sources supporting your claim or thesis. If you have only one research article supporting your view, you may not have gotten the entire picture.

- Use a variety of resources. Some of the best sources can be found in encyclopedias, indexes, abstracts, government documents, and journals.

- Know the validity of the sources and research that you use to justify your position. The credibility of your sources can mean the difference between having a valid argument and having unsubstantiated opinions. With the Internet becoming an ever-increasing and popular source for information, it is extremely important that you know the validity of your Internet resources.

Questioning. You've asked questions all of your life. As a child, you asked your parents "What's that?" a million times. You probably also asked them, "Why do I have to do this?" In more recent years, you've asked questions of your friends, teachers, strangers, store clerks, and significant others. Questioning is not new to you, but it may be a new technique for exploring, developing, acquiring new knowledge, and working with case studies. Your curiosity is one of the most important traits you possess, especially when working with cases. Questions help you gain insight where you may have limited knowledge. They can also challenge you to look at issues from many different angles. Answering properly posed questions can help you expand your knowledge base.

Distinguishing fact from opinion. Your case study may contain both facts and opinions. A *fact* is something that can be proven, or objectively verified. An *opinion* is a statement that is held to be true but that has no objective proof—something that has not been objectively verified. Statements that cannot be proven should always be treated as opinion. Statements that offer valid proof and verification from credible, reliable sources can be treated as factual. If something sounds as if it could be true, but you have no evidence or proof, it is just an opinion.

If you are in doubt whether a statement in the case is fact or opinion, ask questions, conduct research, listen to group members, and work to find solid proof and documentation to support the statement. Also consider the following:

- Listen for what is not said in a statement.
- Don't be led astray by those you assume are trustworthy and loyal.
- Don't be turned off by those you fear or consider untruthful.

■ Do your own homework on the issue. Read, research, and question.

Searching for ambiguous words and phrases. Before you agree with an opinion or fact in your case study, you will need to examine the "real" meaning of key words and phrases in the case. In the course of evaluating your cases, you may run across the following phrases: "There was reasonable cause . . ."; "We suspect that he was . . ."; "It can be inferred that . . ."; "It appears obvious to us that . . ."; "Research suggests that . . ."; and "According to experts . . ." These phrases may have no hidden meaning, but if someone's fate depended on these words, wouldn't you want to know what was actually meant? You might ask such questions as "What research?" "What experts?" "Who suspects what and why?" and "To whom does it appear obvious?" Obtaining the answers to these questions can help eliminate ambiguity in your casework.

Listening. Listening is a survival skill. For many animals, it is necessary to sustain life, through self-defense and obtaining food. For humans, listening is necessary for the establishment of relationships, growth, survival, knowledge, entertainment, and even health. It is one of the most important and widely used tools humans possess. Research suggests that we spend almost 70 percent of our waking time communicating (Adler, 2002). Fifty-three percent of that time is spent in listening situations. Effective listening skills are a vital part of critical thinking and will play an important role in your case study work.

Any of several major obstacles can prevent you from being an effective listener. When working on your cases, strive to overcome the following issues:

■ *Prejudging.* Prejudging is one of the biggest obstacles to active listening. Prejudging means that you automatically shut out what is being said. You may prejudge because of the content or because of the person communicating. Prejudging can also evolve from environment, culture, attitude, social status, or attitude.

■ *Talking.* Not even the best listeners in the world can listen when they themselves are talking. To become an effective listener, learn the power of silence. Silence gives you the opportunity to think, listen, and consider. By being silent, you allow yourself to think about what is being said before you are required to respond. This small amount of time can be invaluable.

■ *Bringing your emotions to the table.* A barrier to active listening is bringing your emotions to the listening situation. As discussed earlier, your emotions can cause you to shut out certain information. Your worries, problems, fears, or anger can prevent you from practicing critical thinking and from listening to the greatest advantage.

PROBLEM SOLVING AND CASE STUDIES

You face problems every day, some larger and more difficult than others. Some students have transportation problems or child care problems, while others have academic or interpersonal problems. Many people don't know how to solve problems at school, home, or work. They simply let the problem go unattended until it is too late to reach a suitable conclusion. Many ways to address and solve problems exist.

When working with your case study, problem solving will be a major component of your work. As you begin to delve into the case's problem(s), consider the following strategies:

Identify and Narrow the Problem

As you begin to work on your case, remember that the most obvious problem may not be the *root* of the problem. Discovering the root of the problem is hard work, and many people choose to deal with symptoms of the problem rather than address the underlying "illness" itself. When reading your case, jot down all aspects of the problem, such as why the problem exists, whom does it affect, and what type of problem is it?

Examine the following situation: You have just failed two tests this week, and you are dreadfully behind on an English paper. Now, that's a problem . . . or is it? If you examine and reflect on the problem, you begin to realize that because of your nighttime job, you always get to class late, you are tired and irritable when you get there, and you never have time to study. So, the real problem (the illness) *is not* that you have failed tests and are behind—those are symptoms. The real problem is that your job is interfering with your college work. Now that you have identified and narrowed the root of the problem, you can begin to work toward a solution.

Develop Alternatives

A valuable method of gathering ideas, formulating questions, and solving problems is brainstorming. To brainstorm, you let your ideas flow without any fear of ridicule. A brainstorming session allows all thoughts to be heard. You can brainstorm any matter almost anywhere. You may want to set the following guidelines for your sessions to make them more productive:

- Identify the topic, problem, or statement to be discussed.
- Set a time limit for the entire brainstorming session.
- Write all ideas down on a board or flip chart.
- Let everyone speak.
- Don't criticize other speakers for their remarks.
- Concentrate on the issues in the case; let all of your ideas flow.

- Suspend judgment until all ideas have been produced or the time is up.
- If you're using the session to generate questions rather than solutions, each participant should pose questions rather than statements.

Evaluate the Alternatives

Some of your ideas or the ideas of your classmates may not be logical in solving the problem(s) presented in the case. After careful study and deliberation, and without emotional interference, analyze the ideas presented and determine whether they are appropriate or inappropriate for the solution.

Offer a Solution to the Problem

Now that you have a few strong alternatives about the case derived from brainstorming, offer what you have determined to be the most logical, rational solution to the problem.

COOPERATIVE LEARNING AND CASE STUDIES

Cooperative learning is learning that takes place among your peers. It occurs when you are actively involved with a group of your classmates in making decisions, determining outcomes, formulating questions, and evaluating solutions. Cooperative learning teams may be assigned by the professor to address the cases presented in this book.

If you are assigned to a cooperative learning team to assist with a case, cultivating a trusting relationship with the other members is essential. In cooperative learning, every student is expected to "pull his or her own weight." You may be assigned a topic to research, an article to bring to the next meeting, or an interview to conduct to assist with the case. Your successful completion of the assigned task will determine that you can be a trusted member of that cooperative learning group.

"Freeloading" is a common problem with cooperative learning. *Freeloading* occurs when team members do not pull their own weight and instead rest on the laurels of the group's other members. Often, freeloaders receive the same grade as those who did the work. This can be distressing, but dealing with a freeloader is a lesson with real-life implications. Freeloading can even be a case study on its own. You may have to do some internal problem solving to deal with freeloaders.

As you work in your cooperative learning team, remember that cooperative learning *is not*:

- A social time
- A gripe or moan session
- A time for slacking off and missing class

- A time to catch up on missed homework
- A time for unstructured activity
- A time for one person to dominate
- A time to embarrass anyone

Cooperative learning *is*:

- A time to work
- A time to express ideas and thoughts
- A time to reflect
- A time to analyze
- A time to share creative ideas
- A time to pull from other's strengths and knowledge
- A time to ask questions
- A time to solve problems
- A time to work together to master material
- A time to gather information

When working in cooperative learning teams, keep the following tips in mind:

- Listen with an open mind.
- Respect the values, ideas, and past experiences of others.
- Give the person speaking your undivided attention.
- Ask questions—and give people time to respond.
- Share your information and experiences.
- Don't dominate the discussion.
- Give constructive criticism, but don't be overly critical.
- Respond and react to ideas, *not* to people.
- Accept plausible suggestions.
- Don't be rude and insensitive, even if you adamantly disagree.

ANALYZING THE CASE

A common mistake with case studies occurs when participants jump into the case without a working plan. Before you begin your first case, consider the following:

- Read through the case first without taking notes, making judgments, or coming to conclusions. Familiarizing yourself with the issues of the case can help you later in the process.

- As mentioned earlier, some cases do not provide all of the information needed. If your cooperative learning team agrees, it is OK to make assumptions about the case as long as it is clearly stated that assumptions have been made.

- To process the case, you may have to rely on your own experiences, the experiences of the group, and the research that each member brings to the group.

- Your research or experiences may not provide enough information to process the case. You may have to make educated guesses and brainstorm to have enough information and insight to process the case.

- When assessing the case, use whatever sources you have to assist you in coming to some conclusions regarding the case. This might include the group's research, personal experiences, trial and error, and experiences from your cooperative learning team.

- Remember that your analysis of this case should be realistic, valuable, and immediately useful.

GUIDELINES FOR ANALYZING YOUR CASE STUDY

As you go through the case, you will encounter many opinions, multiple solutions, and varied approaches to a resolution. Remember, there are no right or wrong answers, only different methods for solving the problems. As you begin working on your case, keep the following guidelines in mind:

- Everyone in the group (if you are working with a group) *must* have read the case at hand.

- Everyone in the group must agree on the circumstances of the case— that is, all members should agree about the basics of the case.

- Work with the facts of the case. Weed out information that you do not need, and concentrate on the important facts of the case.

- Determine what you need to know that is not provided.

- Begin an open discussion that involves every member of the group. Allow all members to cite what they know about the case.

- As the discussion builds, do not argue, judge, or interrupt. You should, however, take notes so that you can come back to a statement that needs clarification by a group member.

- Listen carefully, and avoid becoming emotional.

- As the discussion grows, have one member write down all of the problems associated with the case as mentioned by group members.

- Have the note taker write down any assumptions that may have to be made.

- Narrow the problems down to primary or secondary problems. Discuss why the problems exist. What has caused each of the problems? Is there one person at the root of the problem? Is more than one person involved at the root of the problem? If so, who are they? Why are they "the problem"?
- Discuss each problem listed to find the *root* problem.
- Once the root problem has been agreed on, have each member of the group research possible solutions. This research can be from literature, interviews, and various other sources.
- When the group comes back together, have each member discuss what he found and then brainstorm to come to the most suitable solution.
- Make a recommendation for the appropriate actions.
- Once the solution has been agreed on, discuss the moral and ethical implications of your solution.
- Discuss the consequences of your solution.
- Discuss the implications for the people involved in the case.
- Brainstorm and determine what real-life implications your case study has for students.
- Discuss where students faced with the situation described in your case can find assistance on campus.

GIVE IT A TRY

Go back to the beginning of this chapter and reread the case of Harriett and Belinda. Using the questions below, work to find the most appropriate solution to the case. You will use these questions throughout the remainder of the text.

CLOSING THOUGHTS

Although you may be new to case study learning, you will soon understand how engaging a case analysis can be. You will discover how exciting it can be to learn from your peers' experiences, how advantageous it can be to expand your critical thinking and problem solving skills, and how enjoyable it can be to reach a conclusion through teamwork and mutual cooperation.

References

Adler, R. *Understanding Human Communication,* 8th Edition. Canada: Oxford University Press, 2002.

Helpern, D. *Thought and Knowledge: An Introduction to Critical Thinking.* Mahwah, NJ: Lawrence Earlbaum, 1996.

Case Study Analysis

Name _____   Date _____

Class _____   Section _____

1. What are the **facts** you KNOW about the case?
   _____
   _____
   _____

2. What are some **logical assumptions** you can make about the case?
   _____
   _____
   _____

3. What are the **problems** involved in the case as you see it?
   _____
   _____
   _____

4. What is the **root problem** (the main issue)?
   _____

5. What do you estimate is the **cause of the root problem?**
   _____
   _____

6. What are the **reasons** that the root problem exists?
   _____
   _____
   _____

7. What is (are) the **solution(s)** to the problem?
   _____
   _____
   _____

8. Are there any **moral and/or ethical considerations** to your solution?

_____

_____

_____

9. What are the **consequences** of your solution?

_____

_____

_____

10. What are the **"real-world" implications** for this case?

_____

_____

_____

11. How will the **lives** of the people in the case study **be changed** because of your proposed solution?

_____

_____

_____

12. Where are some **areas on campus** that one could get help with the problems associated with this case?

_____

_____

_____

13. Where are some **areas beyond the campus** that one could get help with the problems associated with this case?

_____

_____

_____

14. What **personal advice** would you give to Harriett?

_____

_____

_____

Creating Positive Change

Change occurs the fastest in your first year of college. Friends change, past relationships change, issues at home change, attitudes change, and teachers change.

Change can be one of the most traumatic experiences of your life, or it can be one of the most exciting times of your life. It all depends on how you deal with change, how you maneuver through change, and whether you learn to view change as a positive force of life or a negative force beyond your control.

CASE 1   So Far Away

Takeshi leaves Japan to study in the United States, where he is planning to fulfill a lifetime dream and receive an education that will prepare him for his future. He has no idea of the culture shock he faces. He is very bright and was a leader in his school in Japan. Suddenly, he is just one of thousands—and one who is "different" from most of the other students. Can he make the changes necessary to survive and thrive in this new and vastly different environment?

CASE 2   Rushing Toward Change

Cameron is excited about going to college and joining a sorority. Having grown up on the East Coast, she arrives on campus at a major university in Louisiana. She is pleased to be getting away from home and looks forward to making her own decisions. She is unprepared for some of the situations she encounters.

CASE 3   We're Not in Kansas Anymore

Sharli leaves home to major in Social Work, never knowing that her entire life will be turned around by a religion professor with shocking ideas, a biology professor who believes that evolution is superior to creation, and a party where she takes her first drink. Her value system is challenged and shaken. Will she survive? Will her dreams of starting a youth religion center come true?

So Far Away

Takeshi left his home in Japan only three weeks ago, but now it feels as if a lifetime has passed. Although he is able to talk to his family daily via e-mail, the culture shock is still overwhelming. Friends and family had told him that great changes were ahead. Many of his family members were educated in the United States, and his parents spent time here. With all of the advice, warnings, and information, Takeshi is still certain that this is the experience he needs to enhance his life and career opportunities. What he finds in the United States, however, is beyond anything he imagined.

In what is the equivalent of the American high school he attended in Japan, Takeshi received high marks, and his TOEFL score is excellent. By all external measures, he is prepared to be here, but internally he feels like an imposter. Takeshi begins to believe that he has made a terrible mistake and that there is no way he should be here studying with all of these other people. Everyone else appears to understand everything the professors say. Everyone else appears to know exactly where he is going. Everyone else appears to be having a wonderful experience—except him. Each night he goes back to his room in the residence hall, and the walls seem to close in on him. The loneliness is overwhelming. He misses his family, his friends, his teachers, and the familiar streets of his hometown. In fact, he misses everything about his life that only three weeks ago he was taking for granted. He remembers wishing to leave Japan quickly so that he could begin his new life in America! Now he regrets ever making the decision to leave home for college.

In e-mail conversations, Takeshi's father encourages him to be strong, to remember his goals, and to understand that other students feel the same way. He encourages Takeshi to get out and meet other people and to talk to his professors. Each time Takeshi finishes reading his father's e-mails, he is convinced to follow his advice, but when he goes out to get involved, he experiences roadblocks that he can't seem to overcome.

Takeshi is afraid to approach his professors because in his high school in Japan, students do not talk to teachers. Even if he has questions or concerns, it is next to impossible to get near his professors before or after class. The classes are huge, some larger than his entire high school back home, and students swarm around the professors like honeybees around a hive. He tries to ask questions in class, but this is another thing so odd and different about college in America. Every day he watches his classmates openly talking, laughing, and even challenging the professor. Takeshi finds this difficult to do because in his culture, students do not speak to their teachers or professors and they definitely do not become familiar enough with them to joke around—they would never, ever challenge them!

Nonetheless Takeshi continues to take his father's advice and decides to go to a new student mixer that is being held the second week of the semester. Instead of helping his situation, this step only makes things worse. The mixer highlights the differences between the other students and him. He dresses differently, his hair is different, and language is an even bigger barrier. In classes, students speak a dialect of English closer to what he studied in school, but when they are together at this mixer, everyone seems to be speaking a "different English." It sounds completely foreign to him. He leaves the mixer afraid, confused, and angry that he thought he could ever succeed at a university in the United States, so far away from home.

The third week does not bring improvement. Things are moving at such a fast pace that Takeshi cannot keep up. He is quickly falling behind. During each class period, he sits in class trying to take notes, but the professors speak so fast that he can't take notes quickly enough. Many professors use LCD projectors and PowerPoint slides, which he has not seen before. In some classes, the lights are turned low, and he can barely see what he is writing.

Takeshi has turned in his first assignments in several of his classes; when he receives them back, his grades are C's or D's. He even has one F. There is no explanation written on his projects as to why he received the low grades, just the grades themselves. When he tries to see the professor who has failed him on his first paper to find out what he is doing wrong and to ask for help on improving the next paper, the professor is quite rude with him. Before Takeshi can fully explain why he is there, the professor tells him that if he plans to study in an American university he had better be prepared to "run with the big dogs!" Takeshi is confused. He thinks, "I'm not even studying veterinary medicine, and there are no dogs in my class." After a moment, he realizes that the professor is not speaking literally, but he has no clue what the professor means about "big dogs."

Takeshi leaves the professor's office disillusioned, confused, hurt, and still angry. He walks home to his residence hall, and for the first time he does not get lost. He sits down at his computer and logs on to his e-mail. His father just happens to be online at the same time so he instant messages him.

"Dad, are you there?"

His father replies, "Yes, Takeshi, I'm here."

"Dad, I want to come home."

Case Study Analysis

Name _____ Date _____

Class _____ Section _____

1. What are the **facts you KNOW** about the case?

   _____
   _____
   _____

2. What are some **logical assumptions** you can make about the case?

   _____
   _____
   _____

3. What are the **problems** involved in the case as you see it?

   _____
   _____
   _____

4. What is the **root problem** (the main issue)?

   _____

5. What do you estimate is the **cause of the root problem**?

   _____
   _____

6. What are the **reasons** that the root problem exists?

   _____
   _____
   _____

7. What is (are) the **solution(s)** to the problem?

   _____
   _____
   _____

8. Are there any **moral and/or ethical considerations** to your solution?

_____

_____

_____

9. What are the **consequences** of your solution?

_____

_____

_____

10. What are the "**real-world**" **implications** for this case?

_____

_____

_____

11. How will the **lives** of the people in the case study **be changed** because of your proposed solution?

_____

_____

_____

12. Where are some **areas on campus** that one could get help with the problems associated with this case?

_____

_____

_____

13. Where are some **areas beyond the campus** that one could get help with the problems associated with this case?

_____

_____

_____

14. What **personal advice** would you give to Takeshi?

_____

_____

_____

Rushing Toward Change

Cameron arrives on campus a week early because she is going through Rush. Rarely has she been this excited about anything, much less something involving school. She has listened to her older friends talk about their sorority lives for years, and now the time has finally come for her to have a chance at all this excitement. She has given very little thought to school itself. Most of her thoughts are focused on pledging a sorority and living the "great life."

Gregarious and outgoing, Cameron adjusts to college life immediately. She goes from room to room meeting girls who are there for Rush. Some seem very much like her, and some appear to be shy and unpolished. She dresses with extra care that night to go to the first party because she knows how important it is to be available and to let yourself "be seen."

When she arrives at the sorority house, she is taken by the huge columns and the Old South aura surrounding the building. She enters and can't believe how beautiful the building is. "This will truly be a dream come true if I can live here," she thinks. Some of the sisters immediately welcome her and take her around the room to meet other people. Cameron is a little nervous because this is so important to her, and she wants to make a good impression. She has been coached by her older friends, and she is grateful for that. The girls appear to like her, although the whole process seems to be a little superficial. She overhears one of the members making fun of one of the girls who just arrived. "Can you believe she showed up here in that get-up? We wouldn't be caught dead with her. She can forget it."

Cameron isn't quite prepared for the viciousness of some of the thinly veiled remarks. "Maybe this particular sorority isn't for me," she thinks. "They are very different from what my friends talked about." Before the evening is over, she is feeling a little let down and disappointed.

The next evening, Cameron again dresses with care and goes to another party. There she again appears to be accepted and liked and feels pretty confident that she will get bids from her two top choices. The girl who had been dressed poorly attends this one, too, and is standing alone by herself. Cameron goes over and talks to her because she seems so lost. The girl, Madison, tells her that she doesn't want to do this. "My mother was in a sorority, and she insists that I join one as well. This isn't for me. I don't care about parties and clothes and all those things that my mother thinks are important. My main interest is science. I want to be a biology professor, and all this seems so frivolous to me," she tells Cameron.

Cameron feels sorry for her as she moves away to another part of the room. While walking away, she thinks that perhaps she shouldn't be seen associating with her too long because she surely is not going to get a bid.

In the next group Cameron encounters, the discussion centers on one of the girl's family's wealth. "We want to get her because her father is loaded. He could build the new wing by himself if he wanted to. I don't like her very much, but who cares if her old man will foot the bill." Cameron is

shocked at this discussion. She herself comes from a family of relatively modest means. It never occurs to her that they would actually discuss one's family's background and wealth . . . in front of others . . . in public. Her confidence and enthusiasm for the entire process begin to wane.

Over the next few days of Rush, she meets some nice girls and some she really doesn't like at all. She begins to have reservations about whether this sorority deal is for her after all. She thinks back to Madison and realizes that she likes her better than anyone else she has met. "She is just herself," Cameron thinks. "She isn't trying to be anything but Madison, and she isn't pretentious."

Even though her enthusiasm is less than it was when she arrived on campus, Cameron still becomes nervous on the day bids are issued. She is elated when bids from her two favorite groups arrive. Since she had always wanted to join a sorority, she decides to pledge. During the next few days, the sisters go everywhere with the pledges, making them do all kinds of things that she thinks are rather silly. "It's all a part of the game," she tells herself. One of the sisters, Dana Morgan, seems particularly obnoxious and unkind. Cameron learns that her father is a very wealthy oilman from Texas and that Dana feels that she can treat anyone however she wants to. Cameron tries to avoid her because she really does not like her behavior toward others. Her values are so different from Cameron's.

Pledge Week is almost over when Cameron finds herself the target of Dana Morgan. Dana is vice president of the sorority and feels very important. Obviously, she enjoys poking fun at other people. Cameron cringes when she hears Dana's loud voice calling her over to her group. Dana appears to be in a particularly vengeful mood that day as she instructs Cameron to go over to Madison and ask her at which thrift shop she found that tacky outfit.

"Oh, I couldn't do that, Dana," Cameron answers. That would hurt her feelings. Madison is really a very nice person, and I just couldn't do that." Dana is provoked.

"Well, you'll do it if you want to belong to this sorority," Dana says sharply. "You see my friends right here, they'll blackball you if I tell them to. So you've got a choice. Do it or get out!"

"Dana," Cameron pleads, "Why would you want me to intentionally hurt another person?"

"I want you to do what I tell you to do. That is all a part of Rush. If you can't deal with that, you can't deal with sisterhood. And let me tell you one other thing, I have many friends in the other sororities on campus, and if you fail here, you fail everywhere."

The other girls begin to chuckle and snicker at Cameron's situation. She hears one of the girls say, "She's not gonna make it. She doesn't have any backbone. She can't even walk over to that ugly girl and joke with her."

"It's now or never, Cameron," Dana says very curtly. Cameron thinks for a moment and takes a few steps toward Madison. She pauses for a moment and then walks toward Madison.

Case Study Analysis

Name _____ Date _____

Class _____ Section _____

1. What are the **facts** you KNOW about the case?

   _____

   _____

   _____

   _____

2. What are some **logical assumptions** you can make about the case?

   _____

   _____

   _____

   _____

3. What are the **problems** involved in the case as you see it?

   _____

   _____

   _____

   _____

4. What is the **root problem** (the main issue)?

   _____

   _____

5. What do you estimate is the **cause of the root problem**?

   _____

   _____

6. What are the **reasons** that the root problem exists?

   _____

   _____

   _____

   _____

7. What is (are) the **solution(s)** to the problem?

   _____

   _____

   _____

8. Are there any **moral and/or ethical considerations** to your solution?

_____

_____

_____

9. What are the **consequences** of your solution?

_____

_____

_____

10. What are the **"real-world" implications** for this case?

_____

_____

_____

11. How will the **lives** of the people in the case study **be changed** because of your proposed solution?

_____

_____

_____

12. Where are some **areas on campus** that one could get help with the problems associated with this case?

_____

_____

_____

13. Where are some **areas beyond the campus** that one could get help with the problems associated with this case?

_____

_____

_____

14. What **personal advice** would you give to Cameron?

_____

_____

_____

We're Not in Kansas Anymore

Sharli is seriously involved with her church, so when it is announced that the congregation will be throwing her a graduation and going away party, it is not much of a surprise to her or her family. Sharli is the first in her family to go to college and also one of the only people in her small town's church to ever go. Sharli won a scholarship to the University of Pennsylvania to study Social Work. Her dream is to return home, become a social worker, and start a youth religion center in her community.

In late August, Sharli arrives on campus and begins the difficult task of moving into the residence hall, meeting her roommates, attending orientation, registering for classes, and trying to forget that she is so homesick that she has been fighting back tears for hours. "I'm not going to give up," she says to herself. "There is too much riding on this."

After classes start, Sharli begins to feel more at home and more at ease being several hundred miles away from everything she knows and loves. She meets several acquaintances through the Organization of Student Social Workers and the Campus Connection, a religious club. Things are finally going well.

Sharli registers for five classes: English 101, History 110, Biology 101, Cultural Anthropology 101, and Religious Studies 112. The classes are challenging, but Sharli is pulling an A or B in every class except Religious Studies. It is disheartening to her that she is not doing well in a class that is so close to her heart and nature. The class has been hard since the first day.

"My name is Dr. Walter Campbell," the professor says on the first day. "This is Religious Studies, and you are here to learn how to think for yourselves, how to debunk the myths of the Bible, how to critically examine your beliefs, and how to find critical essay on religion in the library." Everyone is very quiet. "We are not here for church. I am not your preacher. I am not your counselor. I say to you that by the end of this semester, you will have reevaluated everything you think you know about God, Jesus, Buddha, Muhammad, and yourself." Sharli feels her heart pounding in her chest, almost choking her. Dr. Campbell gives out the syllabus, details the work that will be done, and dismisses the class. Sharli and some of her classmates are breathless as they leave.

As the semester progresses, the content of the course becomes harder and Dr. Campbell more illogical, in Sharli's mind. If a student makes a comment about religion or the Bible, Dr. Campbell yells, "Prove it!" or "Says who?" or "That's about as untrue as a politician on election day." There seems to be no pleasing him. Sharli and 80 percent of the class fail the first test. She is lost in a world that has given her so much pleasure in the past.

Biology is going better, but the professor requires that every student purchase *On the Origin of Species* by Charles Darwin. The professor, Dr.

Margie Vanier, pushes the concept that living things did not come from God's special creation but, rather, evolved out of earlier forms that lived at an earlier time, hence the Theory of Evolution. Sharli's minister back home often speaks of evolution and calls it "man's attempt to scientifically explain faith." Until this class, Sharli has never read about evolution and has certainly never heard anyone in person discount the Bible's theory of creation. Sharli grows more confused by the moment.

Cultural Anthropology is an interesting class, and the professor is a nonconfrontational, easygoing young man from Australia. While interesting, Anthropology also poses a "threat" to some of Sharli's firmly planted beliefs. It seems as if there is no place to turn without controversy and a feeling of walking on eggshells. There are days when all she wants is to call home and tell her mother to come and get her. But she knows in her heart that she is meant for more.

Socially, Sharli has made several new friends through classes and clubs. They often gather in one another's rooms for pizza, conversation, and studying. It is at one of the pizza study sessions that Sharli takes the first drink of her life. Her friends have brought beer to the room, and everyone seems to be having such a good time. Before she realizes it, she is dizzy and laughing with delight. This will not be the last time that Sharli takes a drink. It becomes a regular event on Thursday evenings.

As the semester progresses, Sharli feels more and more as if she is "at home." She actually looks forward to going to Dr. Campbell's Religious Studies class. She is even shocked by the fact that she finds him to be an interesting man with an interesting perspective. Still, she is not doing that well on the assigned papers, but her grades have improved. Dr. Vanier's lectures on evolution are difficult to comprehend, but rationally, Sharli begins to understand the concept. Her close circle of friends grows, and she begins to go out and party with them more frequently. Life is good except for one thing. Sharli cannot shake a feeling of overwhelming, crushing guilt.

She believes that she is at the University of Pennsylvania to learn more about the world and religion and people and cultures and traditions, but she is not prepared for all of the things that are coming her way. In her mind, she begins to seriously wonder if her small town's religious training has been in error and if her minister is correct about his teachings. This scares her right down to the core. She wonders if evolution is more logical than creation. "Is there really a God who made us all?" she wonders. "Are there really people on earth who will never accept God as a divine entity?"

She is drinking every week, sometimes two or three times a week, and she is going to places she knows her mama would not approve of. The guilt is almost paralyzing. Sharli is having the time of her life, but she feels as if

she is abandoning and betraying her past. She is confused and scared. Her
entire value system has been rattled. She is seriously considering transferring
to the community college near her home. "Maybe things will be easier
there," she thinks. "Maybe I will not be so confused and guilty." In her mind
she knows that if she goes home, she could return to her church on Sundays.

There is only one person to whom she can talk.

Sharli sits on the edge of her bed and dials the phone.

"Hi, Mama, this is Sharli."

Case Study Analysis

Name _____   Date _____

Class _____   Section _____

1. What are the **facts** you KNOW about the case?

_____

_____

_____

2. What are some **logical assumptions** you can make about the case?

_____

_____

_____

3. What are the **problems** involved in the case as you see it?

_____

_____

_____

4. What is the **root problem** (the main issue)?

_____

_____

5. What do you estimate is the **cause of the root problem**?

_____

_____

6. What are the **reasons** that the root problem exists?

_____

_____

_____

7. What is (are) the **solution(s)** to the problem?

_____

_____

_____

8. Are there any **moral and/or ethical considerations** to your solution?

_____

_____

_____

9. What are the **consequences** of your solution?

_____

_____

_____

10. What are the **"real-world" implications** for this case?

_____

_____

_____

11. How will the **lives** of the people in the case study **be changed** because of your proposed solution?

_____

_____

_____

12. Where are some **areas on campus** that one could get help with the problems associated with this case?

_____

_____

_____

13. Where are some **areas beyond the campus** that one could get help with the problems associated with this case?

_____

_____

_____

14. What **personal advice** would you give to Sharli?

_____

_____

_____

Discovering
Resources

It is suggested that students who make contact with three other people on a college campus are more likely to remain at that institution. Those three people are another student who can be trusted, a faculty member who cares for your well-being, and a staff person who knows how to get things done. Campus resources involve more than buildings . . . They also involve people.

CASE 1 Reach Out and Touch

Becky had attended a large urban high school where she had a group of seven friends who had been her main support network. This group had worked for her election as student body vice president. Her best friend had assisted her in getting a great summer job with a boss who had been an excellent mentor. Her drama teacher had been instrumental in getting her involved in the local theater group. When she leaves for a large university in another state, she leaves this network behind. Suddenly, Becky finds herself alone and struggling without this network.

CASE 2 Free at Last, Free at Last!

Jonathan leaves his small rural midwestern community for a large university because he has an intense desire to experience a lifestyle very different from the one he has had as teenager in a small rural community. He wants excitement and fulfillment, even though he doesn't know what it will take to excite or fulfill him. He just knows it isn't happening where he is, so he goes on a journey to find an exciting and fulfilling life at the university.

CASE 3 Give Me Credit . . . Please!

Resa is a mother of twins who will be entering kindergarten this fall. For the first time in years, she has the opportunity to attend college. She has saved a little money, but not enough to pay for tuition and books. She is working full-time but has decided to move to part-time in order to concentrate on her degree. She is awarded a small grant and decides to charge the rest of her education on several new credit cards. Shortly into the semester, her car breaks and she is forced to draw a cash advance to pay for the car. Will Resa's ever-increasing debt load cost her her dream?

Reach Out and Touch

Becky is a new first-year student at Stapleton College, a highly respected school on the East Coast. She selects this school because of its reputation in her chosen field and because she is awarded a full scholarship. Although she is very excited about the opportunity, she arrives from Oregon feeling more than a little lost. She has left behind her support group—the Magnificent Seven, they called themselves—and she is beginning to realize how important they, and some of her favorite teachers, have been to her. She even misses her boss from her summer job who has been a mentor for her.

As she walks through campus on a beautiful fall day, Becky begins to wonder if she should have gone to school so far from home. She thinks about her friends often, and she is having a difficult time engaging herself in her courses. Over the past few days, she has been really tempted to call her parents and tell them she wants to come home.

After several days of moping around, Becky decides that she is not going to give up. She realizes that the past is over and that she has to build a new network of support. When she has time to think about it, she tries to formulate a plan. She tries to answer recurring questions about the kinds of support she needs. "Where do I start?" she asks herself. "Where can I find people who need me and people I can help?"

Becky has chosen Government and International Studies as her major, so she decides to start with her academic advisor for advice. As she always did in high school, Becky drops by Dr. Freeman's office after her Math class. She is more than a little stunned when Dr. Freeman tells her that she will have to have an appointment to meet with her. She explains that she is working on a research paper that has to be finished this week. "Becky, this is not high school," Dr. Freeman says. You can't just drop by my office without an appointment."

"So much for helpful teachers!" Becky thinks to herself.

As she walks briskly down the hall and out of the building, Becky feels hot tears in her eyes and her homesickness is overwhelming. She longs for the Magnificent Seven and Mrs. Todd, her high school drama teacher. To top it all off, Becky realizes that she has to find a way to supplement the allowance her parents are sending her. She knows that they cannot afford to send her more money, because her sister is also in college, and Becky doesn't want her parents to worry about her.

She decides to apply for three jobs on campus, only to be disappointed by finding out that juniors and seniors with more experience have already been given the jobs despite the fact that she has excellent computer skills. She can hardly hold back the tears as she goes back to her room to study.

"Like I can really study with this roommate I've been assigned," she thinks. She has never been exposed to anyone like Marilyn.

Becky has heard horror stories about "roommates from hell," but now she knows they really do exist. Marilyn has come to school to party and meet guys. She has made it absolutely clear that she has no intention of staying at Stapleton but intends to have a good time before she flunks out. Becky asks her nicely to please be more considerate and quiet so she can study.

Becky has been studying for a few moments when there is a knock on the door. Before she can open the door, in walk several of Marilyn's home-town friends. Becky knows she can never study in this environment so she gathers up her materials and walks out amid the taunts of her roommate's gang. On her way to the library, she tries to focus on solutions to her problems. "I've got to get myself together, formulate a plan, and build a support group," she thinks. "I've got to do this."

The next week, things seem to look a little better. One of her classmates invites her to attend the football game along with her boyfriend and his roommate. Not much for blind dates, Becky finally decides to go because she needs to make friends and she loves football. Her date, George, is a mis-take from the beginning. She has actually never seen anyone in Oregon who has quite as many tattoos and body piercings as he does. Although the group goes to dinner after the game, Becky begs off and returns to her room. "Can't I do anything right anymore?" she thinks. "I wonder what the Magnificent Seven are doing tonight? Maybe I should have stayed there, where I was safe."

Drawing on her theatrical experience, Becky goes to the tryouts for the new play. She knows she can play the lead role because she has starred in this play before. She knows she can do an excellent job! She learns after she arrives that the president of the Drama Club wants the lead role, and most people appear to back off from competing with her. "So how do I handle this?" she wonders.

"I've got a roommate from hell, a professor who won't see me without an appointment made a week in advance, a blind date that didn't turn out so well, and a bummer audition for a play on campus," she thinks to her-self. "This is just not what I wanted college to be like," she bemoans. "I thought it would be different. I thought I would feel good about myself and about being here. I just can't seem to fit in."

As she lies in bed that evening smelling cigarette smoke and listening to two people snore on the floor beneath her, she thinks, "Tomorrow, I'll call my friends, 'The 7,' and maybe I'll just go home. Maybe that's what I need to do."

Case Study Analysis

Name _____   Date _____

Class _____   Section _____

1. What are the **facts** you KNOW about the case?

   _____

   _____

   _____

2. What are some **logical assumptions** you can make about the case?

   _____

   _____

   _____

3. What are the **problems** involved in the case as you see it?

   _____

   _____

   _____

4. What is the **root problem** (the main issue)?

   _____

   _____

5. What do you estimate is the **cause of the root problem**?

   _____

   _____

6. What are the **reasons** that the root problem exists?

   _____

   _____

   _____

7. What is (are) the **solution(s)** to the problem?

   _____

   _____

   _____

8. Are there any **moral and/or ethical considerations** to your solution?

_____

_____

_____

9. What are the **consequences** of your solution?

_____

_____

_____

10. What are the **"real-world" implications** for this case?

_____

_____

_____

11. How will the **lives** of the people in the case study **be changed** because of your proposed solution?

_____

_____

_____

12. Where are some **areas on campus** that one could get help with the problems associated with this case?

_____

_____

13. Where are some **areas beyond the campus** that one could get help with the problems associated with this case?

_____

_____

_____

14. What **personal advice** would you give to Becky?

_____

_____

_____

Free at Last, Free at Last!

FREEDOM! Jonathan can smell it; he can taste it as he watches his parents drive away from him at the end of the parents' portion of orientation weekend. He has dreamed of this day for the past three years of high school. "Finally," Jonathan thinks, "I am a first-year student at a Big 10 university!" During orientation he learns that 35,000 students attend his university, 6,000 of which are first-year students like him. He wonders if all of them have the same exhilarating sense of freedom that he does.

It isn't that he doesn't like his parents or that he has a bad life at home; it is the fact that he had been forced to live a life that he considers "boring." Jonathan has lived his entire life in a small farming community in the Midwest, where he attended a small rural high school with the same kids he went to school with his entire life.

As a sophomore in high school, his English teacher, Miss Palorez, challenged him to set goals for his life; that was when he decided to attend a Big 10 university and lead an exciting life. Jonathan wants the freedom to do all the things he imagines people who live outside of small rural towns in the Midwest do. Having never traveled outside of his county, he doesn't know what those things are, but he is determined to find out and then do them!

The three years since Miss Palorez's challenge have quickly passed, and here he is moving into his residence hall, meeting new friends, and attending classes. He has so many opportunities to explore things that he never had a chance to try in his high school. During orientation, he joins several student organizations and writes the times and dates for their meetings in his notebook. Jonathan also meets a professor who gives a session during orientation on "priority management" who is from the college in which he wants to complete his major. After the session, Jonathan approaches Dr. McIntire and asks if they can get together and talk about potential majors. Dr. McIntire agrees but says she is going to be out of town at a conference for a week and then has appointments, so she can't meet for three weeks. They choose a date and time and exchange telephone numbers.

The first week of classes is a whirlwind. Against his academic advisor's recommendations, Jonathan registers for 18 credit hours, because he is certain he can handle the workload. One reason he is just barely handling it, though, is because every night he is meeting new and wonderfully exciting people. First, there are the people in his residence hall, who are incredible. He has never laughed so hard or partied so much in all his life. It is like senior week in high school, only it happens every day and every night and there are no parents to answer to when you come in at night and no parents nagging you about classes the next morning.

The second week of classes is just as crazy. Now the fraternities are starting to talk to him about Rush. Jonathan knows that the people in the fraternities and sororities—the "Greeks"—run the university, so he really

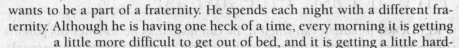

wants to be a part of a fraternity. He spends each night with a different fraternity. Although he is having one heck of a time, every morning it is getting a little more difficult to get out of bed, and it is getting a little harder to stay awake through every class. In fact, today during Art History, Dr. Hasshan actually dropped a book on his desk to wake him up. Jonathan had been so embarrassed, and all the guys from the fraternities had laughed and patted him on the back after class. Jonathan had been mortified and had found Dr. Hasshan in his office later in the day to apologize for falling asleep in class.

By the third week, Jonathan is finding it difficult to make it to class. Tuesday morning his alarm clock goes off. He turns over and hits the snooze but inadvertently hits the off button and falls back to sleep for another four hours. When he wakes up and realizes what has happened, he quickly calls his professor to apologize.

"Dr. Wheelcrest, this is Jonathan Wilson. I'm in your 8:30 class this morning, and somehow my alarm clock messed up. I think it must be broken. Did I miss anything important?" Jonathan asks plaintively.

"Jonathan," Dr. Wheelcrest answers, "if you read your syllabus you would know that I don't take attendance. It is up to you whether or not you put a priority on college and choose to attend your classes. I really could care less whether you are there or not. I only want students sitting in front of me who really want to learn. And as to your question of whether or not you missed anything important, Jonathan"—there is a long pause, and Jonathan wonders if he has lost connection with the professor before Dr. Wheelcrest continues—"no, Jonathan, you didn't miss anything important today. Today I decided to waste both your classmates' time and my time by spending an hour and 15 minutes doing absolutely nothing of use. I'll see you in class on Wednesday, Jonathan." Dr. Wheelcrest hangs up.

Jonathan places the phone in the receiver and is amazed. "Dr. Wheelcrest sure is an odd duck, that joke was kind of funny, but wow—professors who don't care if you are in class," he thought. "I've hit pay dirt." His feelings of good fortune continue until Dr. Wheelcrest's next class, when he greets the students with the words all students hate, "pop quiz."

By the end of the third week, Jonathan is feeling incredibly worn down; in fact he is certain he has the flu, but he can't rest because his parents are coming in for the weekend Not only is it a home game but it is parents' weekend. His father has called several times in the past weeks hinting that his mother is suffering from the "empty nest syndrome," so he knows that there isn't a snowball's chance that they are going to miss this opportunity to visit him. In a way, Jonathan is relieved to see them. "Maybe I can just go to their hotel room and sleep uninterrupted for a day," he thinks. But there is no such luck.

Jonathan opens the door, and his parents greet him with smiles and hugs.

"How are you, Son?" his father asks. "This place looks pretty exciting."

"Give me a kiss, Johnny!" his mom yells. Jonathan does so as he looks around to see if anyone sees them.

"Now, I want to see all of your classes and meet as many of your·professors as I can," his mom says. "I brought the video camera so Grandma Sawyer can see where you live and who's teaching you."

"Mom, they are just regular rooms," Jonathan tries to reason.

"They are not regular to us," his mom insists. "This is your life, and we want to show everyone what you're doing."

Jonathan realizes that this weekend is going to be harder than he thought. But he also realizes that it is good to see his parents for the first time in over a month.

His mother insists on recording his entire college experience on the video camera so that she can send it to family members. When his parents ask him how he is doing in school, Jonathan can't tell them the truth—he can't bring himself to give voice to his innermost doubts—so he just replies, "Everything is great!" and goes on to tell them numerous stories about all of the wonderfully exciting people and things he is experiencing here at the Big 10 university. He doesn't get a moment's rest until he puts them on the plane Sunday evening.

When he returns to his residence hall, he sees that his answering machine's little red light is blinking. He contemplates ignoring it but then decides to listen to his messages. There are two from study groups that he needs to meet with him for group projects, one from a study partner he has blown off on a project that is overdue (needless to say that is a call he was dreading), three from fraternities, and one from Dr. McIntire.

Jonathan plays Dr. McIntire's message: "Jonathan, you missed our appointment we had scheduled for Friday morning in my office at 10:00 A.M. I've rescheduled an appointment for you on Monday at 3:30 P.M. If you would like to see me, please call me at 897-3334 and leave me a message letting me know if you want the appointment."

Jonathan picks up the phone and dials Dr. McIntire's number. When her machine picks up, he says "Dr. McIntire, this is Jonathan. I'd like to . . ."

Case Study Analysis

Name _____ Date _____

Class _____ Section _____

1. What are the **facts** you KNOW about the case?
   _____
   _____
   _____

2. What are some **logical assumptions** you can make about the case?
   _____
   _____
   _____

3. What are the **problems** involved in the case as you see it?
   _____
   _____
   _____

4. What is the **root problem** (the main issue)?
   _____
   _____

5. What do you estimate is the **cause of the root problem**?
   _____
   _____

6. What are the **reasons** that the root problem exists?
   _____
   _____
   _____

7. What is (are) the **solution(s)** to the problem?
   _____
   _____
   _____

8. Are there any **moral and/or ethical considerations** to your solution?

9. What are the **consequences** of your solution?

10. What are the "**real-world**" **implications** for this case?

11. How will the **lives** of the people in the case study **be changed** because of your proposed solution?

12. Where are some **areas on campus** that one could get help with the problems associated with this case?

13. Where are some **areas beyond the campus** that one could get help with the problems associated with this case?

14. What **personal advice** would you give to Jonathan?

Give Me Credit . . . Please!

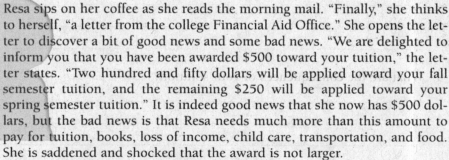

Resa sips on her coffee as she reads the morning mail. "Finally," she thinks to herself, "a letter from the college Financial Aid Office." She opens the letter to discover a bit of good news and some bad news. "We are delighted to inform you that you have been awarded $500 toward your tuition," the letter states. "Two hundred and fifty dollars will be applied toward your fall semester tuition, and the remaining $250 will be applied toward your spring semester tuition." It is indeed good news that she now has $500 dollars, but the bad news is that Resa needs much more than this amount to pay for tuition, books, loss of income, child care, transportation, and food. She is saddened and shocked that the award is not larger.

Resa thinks about what she will do to find the rest of the money to attend college and still be able to take care of her family. Her twins, Thomas and Annie, begin kindergarten this year. For the first time since their birth, she will have some time to spend on her dream of becoming a nurse. "With the twins in school," she thinks to herself, "I can leave my full-time job and find other work on Tuesday and Thursday and go to classes on Monday, Wednesday, and Friday." But now, her dream is threatened because she has saved only $1,000 toward her tuition, and this money, along with the $500 financial aid award, will not even cover the fall semester's tuition.

Determined to make this work, Resa approaches her supervisor on Monday morning to ask if he will allow her to move to part-time status and maintain her health benefits. Mr. Jamison has been very good to Resa over the past three years, and she trusts that he will help her. After lunch, he tells Resa that he has checked with Human Resources and found that she can move to part-time, but that her health benefits will be canceled. This adds another blow to Resa's plans for college.

On Wednesday after work, Resa stops by the Financial Aid Office of the college to talk about scholarships, work-study, other grants, and guaranteed student loans. Before she leaves, she discovers that she can apply for a nursing scholarship after her first semester if she maintains a 3.0 average. She takes the time to apply for a guaranteed student loan while she is in the office. However, the financial aid clerk tells Resa that her loan will not be processed in time for the semester to begin. "Because you're so late in applying," the clerk tells her, "it will probably be mid-October before your money gets here. You'll have to pay your tuition up front, and your check will come later." Another blow!

As Resa leaves the college, she passes a message board and something catches her eye. "This is the answer," she thinks. "It is only temporary, and I make it work with a credit card." She takes several credit card applications from different companies off the board and discovers that they are all offering low interest rates to students. Two of them say that they "Guarantee Approval" for students.

Resa has never applied for a credit card, but she reasons that she can pay her tuition with the card and then pay off the card when the student loan check arrives in October. She fills out the applications that evening, and within two weeks, she has $6,500 in credit. The credit card companies were very generous to her because she has been working full-time for years. Her credit is also spotless.

As the semester approaches, Resa pays her tuition with her savings, her financial aid award, and her new credit card. She buys her books and supplies and pays her Cobra insurance plan with a cash advance from the cards. When all is said and done, Resa charges or cash advances $4,100. She is frightened at owing that much money, but it was the only way that she could make it work.

Classes are going well. Resa works two days per week, spends time with her children, even studying alongside them frequently. Finances are tight, but the family is making it. She has cut back on many expenses, including cable TV, movies, eating out, and her weekly nail appointment.

As Resa leaves for school on Wednesday morning, she notices a huge puddle under her car. She opens the hood and looks around but does not see anything. She loads the twins in the car and drops them off three blocks away. She continues for a moment longer, until smoke begins to billow from under the hood. As the car grinds to a halt, she pulls over only to discover later that her engine block has cracked. Since this is her only transportation, she is desperate.

Later that evening, the garage calls to let her know that to repair the car, she will have to have a new engine. The mechanic tells Resa that she can get a used engine for about $2,500. Stunned, she asks if there is any other alternative. The mechanic assures her that her engine is dead. She decides to pull the last $100 from her savings, and she uses her credit cards to cash advance the remaining $2,400. Resa has now "maxed out" her cards and spent her savings, and the monthly bills are beginning to come in. Her financial aid loan will not arrive for another four weeks.

When she gets to school on Friday, she discovers that a deposit of $100 is due for the nursing outfit she will need for next semester's internship. Panic sets in as she begins to wonder if she has made the right decision. Her financial worries are beginning to take a toll on her stress level, her relationships with her children, and her studying habits. She finds that she is edgy, quick to anger, and constantly frustrated.

As Resa leaves the Student Union on Friday afternoon, she walks by the message board to see if any part-time, weekend jobs are posted. She does not see any jobs posted this week. However, her eye catches a credit card application from another company. The word "GUARANTEED!" is spelled out in big, bright red letters. She reaches for the colored flyer, puts it in her purse, and leaves campus.

Case Study Analysis

Name _____   Date _____

Class _____   Section _____

1. What are the **facts** you KNOW about the case?

_____

_____

_____

2. What are some **logical assumptions** you can make about the case?

_____

_____

_____

3. What are the **problems** involved in the case as you see it?

_____

_____

_____

_____

4. What is the **root problem** (the main issue)?

_____

_____

5. What do you estimate is the **cause of the root problem**?

_____

_____

6. What are the **reasons** that the root problem exists?

_____

_____

_____

7. What is (are) the **solution(s)** to the problem?

_____

_____

_____

8. Are there any **moral and/or ethical considerations** to your solution?

_____

_____

_____

9. What are the **consequences** of your solution?

_____

_____

_____

10. What are the **"real-world" implications** for this case?

_____

_____

_____

11. How will the **lives** of the people in the case study **be changed** because of your proposed solution?

_____

_____

_____

12. Where are some **areas on campus** that one could get help with the problems associated with this case?

_____

_____

_____

13. Where are some **areas beyond the campus** that one could get help with the problems associated with this case?

_____

_____

_____

14. What **personal advice** would you give to Resa?

_____

_____

_____

Relationships and Communication

One's ability to communicate and get along with others goes far beyond the classroom, places of worship, and the home; it goes into the world. Communication is the single most important skill that any human can possess. Employers seek people with effective communication and human relationship skills at every turn.

3

CASE 1   The Pursuit of Happiness . . . Maybe

Sonya is returning to college after a 15-year absence. She is worried about fitting in, attending to her family's needs, and doing well as a student. School goes very well for Sonya as she meets new friends and begins a new life. But all is not well at home. Her husband does not support her college endeavors and does not seem to support her dreams in general.

CASE 2   Only the Lonely

When Sal leaves for college, he knows that it will be hard. However, he does not realize how hard it will be until he has to face his first round of holidays without family or friends. This is doubly hard for Sal because the Jewish holidays happen within the first four weeks of school. Sal has not had a chance to establish a network of friends. In fact, he doesn't know another Jewish person at his university. To make matters worse, the nearest synagogue that he knows of is way off campus and he doesn't want to go to services alone. Sal has not connected with a single soul on campus, which is exactly the opposite of his experience in high school in New York City, where he grew up. The loneliness and sense of isolation Sal is experiencing are overwhelming and about to get the better of him.

CASE 3   I Love You to Death

Richard and Deborah meet in first-year orientation. Shortly afterward, they begin dating. Things are going well until Deborah is assigned a group project with several male students. Richard becomes enraged that she enjoys their company as much as his. He confronts her one evening about her behavior with the male group members and even grabs her arm. Disgusted with Richard, she leaves him only to take him back a few days later. Will she regret her decision?

The Pursuit of Happiness . . . Maybe

Sonya is a mother of three, a wife, a daughter, an aunt, a part-time clerical assistant and, finally, a student. She has returned to college after a 15-year absence. She began college after high school but left after she got married and had her first child, Jeremy. She later had two other children, Sarah and Mack. This is Mack's first year in all-day kindergarten, which frees Sonya to return to school.

Sonya is very, very nervous as she goes through the registration process, orientation, and first day of class. She realizes that she is much older than many college students and wonders if she will make any friends and feel connected or if her fear of isolation will come true. Sonya has a winsome personality and is bright, but she worries about the age, cultural, social, and attitude differences.

As Sonya enters her first class, Sociology 101, she is relieved that she is not the only "older" person in the class. The class has three women and two men around her age. The younger students don't seem to mind that they are there, which also surprises Sonya.

Before the professor comes in, Sonya and a few classmates begin to chat. This relieves her tension and stress even more. Barry, Doug, and Kamal are Sonya's age, and Colleen, Leo, and April are in their late teens. They introduce themselves and share war stories about registration, fees, and parking.

When the professor enters, a hush falls over the class. He calls the roll, goes over the syllabus, and talks about the class in general. He states that the class will be interactive and that everyone will participate in discussions, debates, and presentations. Everyone seems a little shocked, but Professor Elliott seems friendly and approachable. At the end of class, Sonya says good-bye to her new acquaintances and heads off to English 101.

As Sonya enters English 101, she is delighted to find that Leo and Kamal are in the same class. They sit together and talk about Dr. Elliott's Sociology class and his expectations of them. Another student, Brian, overhears them and turns to ask a few questions about Dr. Elliott since he is enrolled in another section of Dr. Elliott's Sociology class. They discuss the first day with Brian until Professor Carrigan enters. The professor begins to talk about the requirements for the class and the importance of attendance and writing in the daily journals.

As Sonya leaves for the day, she is delighted that the classes went so well and that she met a few people who seem nice and friendly. She is even more delighted that she met people her age and that they were all accepted by the younger students. This was a complete surprise to her.

Sonya goes home and begins to prepare dinner, straighten the house, and get ready for the children and her husband to come home. Currently an investment broker with a major firm, her husband completed a degree in Business Administration shortly after their first child was born.

After the children are settled in for the evening, the dishes washed, and clothes arranged for the next day, Sonya relaxes with her husband in the den.

She shares her day with him and tells him about her classes, her professors, and the other students she met. Charlie, her husband, listens to her, but she sees a distant look on his face. He does not want her to be in college right now because he fears that she might neglect the children or lose her part-time job. She assures him again that things will be fine and that for the first time in years, she feels as if she is living her *own* life again, not just living for others.

The semester progresses well for Sonya. Her grades are good, she feels excited and challenged, she enjoys the company of her new friends, and she is looking forward to taking more classes. The only problem is on the home front. Charlie has grown increasingly jealous of her time in study groups with Kamal, Barry, Leo, April, and the others. Sonya has never neglected her children or her home life, but Charlie continually gives her a hard time about spending her spare time with "those people."

As the semester progresses, Sonya and her friends are faced with several major projects. They have a group presentation due in Sociology, and Sonya has a major paper due for English. She decides to have the group over to her home to work on the group presentation. She invites Kamal to bring her son so that he can play with her children while they work. She plans to order pizza for everyone as they work on their presentation.

When she informs Charlie about her plans, he goes ballistic. He demands that she cancel the study group and tells her that she is never to have "those strangers" in the house. She explains to him that she knows them well and that they must work together on the Sociology project. He demands that she take care of her school business at school and not to bring it home.

To keep the peace at home, she calls the group and tells them that she has had a family emergency and will not be able to meet. The next Monday in class, the group agrees to meet at a local restaurant to complete the Sociology project. Sonya informs Charlie that she is going to a study group, that she has made arrangements for the children, and that she will not be home for dinner. Charlie questions her further about where she is going and why, and reminds her that he told her to keep her schoolwork at school. She reasons with him that her grade is on the line and that she must attend the meeting to work on the project.

Sonya drops the children off at her sister's home and drives to the restaurant. Barry, Doug, Kamal, and Colleen are already seated in a back corner of the restaurant. Shortly after Sonya arrives, Leo and April come in. They order several appetizers and talk about their project. The conversation leads to personal topics, world issues, college gossip, and catching up in general. Sonya feels alive and vibrant. She is discussing issues that she has not thought about in years. "For the first time in ten years," she thinks, "I'm growing."

As the discussion, laughter, and jovial conversation continue, Sonya looks toward the front door of the restaurant to see Charlie enter. He looks around the room and heads toward the table.

Case Study Analysis

Name _____   Date _____

Class _____   Section _____

1. What are the **facts** you KNOW about the case?
   _____
   _____
   _____
   _____

2. What are some **logical assumptions** you can make about the case?
   _____
   _____
   _____
   _____

3. What are the **problems** involved in the case as you see it?
   _____
   _____
   _____
   _____

4. What is the **root problem** (the main issue)?
   _____

5. What do you estimate is the **cause of the root problem**?
   _____
   _____

6. What are the **reasons** that the root problem exists?
   _____
   _____
   _____

7. What is (are) the **solution(s)** to the problem?
   _____
   _____

8. Are there any **moral and/or ethical considerations** to your solution?

_____

_____

_____

9. What are the **consequences** of your solution?

_____

_____

_____

10. What are the **"real-world" implications** for this case?

_____

_____

_____

11. How will the **lives** of the people in the case study **be changed** because of your proposed solution?

_____

_____

_____

12. Where are some **areas on campus** that one could get help with the problems associated with this case?

_____

_____

_____

13. Where are some **areas beyond the campus** that one could get help with the problems associated with this case?

_____

_____

_____

14. What **personal advice** would you give to Sonya?

_____

_____

_____

Only the Lonely

Today is Rosh Hashanah, and the loneliness that Sal is experiencing washes over him much like the river he and his family always visits. They visit the river on the first afternoon of the Jewish holiday to empty their pockets into the water, symbolizing the "casting off" of their sins. The river is just one of the many traditions he is going to miss this new year. He is not going to spend the day in the synagogue with his family, nor is he going to share any of the traditional meals of dipping apples and bread into honey symbolizing their wishes for a sweet new year. All of these traditions he will miss, just as he had missed the traditions surrounding Yom Kippur several days ago. On Yom Kippur, Sal had dressed in the traditional white clothing and spent the day fasting and reading the traditional prayers quietly in his room. He spent the day alone because he has not yet found a synagogue close to the campus, nor has he found any other Jewish friends.

It was on Yom Kippur that he overheard his roommate, John, and his friend Ayako talking about him as they were leaving his room.

John said, "Ayako, did you check out Sal's clothes? They were wack."

"Yea, dude, that guy's sick," replied Ayako as they reached the elevator. "The dude is just so out there, so quiet and into his own stuff man—it's like nothing I've ever seen. All this meditation, Gandhi-type stuff with the white clothes, and not eating. I mean I know he's Jewish, but I've never seen a Jew who is so into the religion."

Things between John and Sal had not been all that great before Yom Kippur. Granted, Sal's eavesdropping on the conversation between John and Ayako through a door did not help the matter. Now he has been obsessing for some time over what he thought he heard during this conversation. The thought of them talking about him hurts his feelings and continues to feed his feelings of isolation and loneliness. Sal now believes that John thinks he is odd and is talking to his friends about him as his roommate the "cult member."

Sal thinks he and John are as opposite from each other as two people can be. John is from Los Angeles, California. Sal is from New York City. John is an only child, and Sal is from a large family with lots of extended family. John likes to party all night, while Sal is more studious. John likes to stay up late and sleep late, while Sal goes to bed around 11:00 P.M. to midnight and gets up at 8:00 A.M. Although Sal tried to make friends with John at the beginning of the semester, it has quickly become clear that there is very little common ground between the two of them and the most they can hope for is a peaceful coexistence.

While Sal is sitting in his room thinking about the day ahead, the phone rings.

"Hello," Sal says.

"L'shana tovah tikatev v'taihatem, my son."

Hearing the traditional Hebrew greeting for Rosh Hashanah, which means "May you be inscribed and sealed for a good year," is indeed balm to Sal's troubled soul.

"L'shana tovah tikatev v'taihatem, to you as well, Papa," says Sal. "I was just thinking about you and the family and our trips to the river. I'm feeling so lonely, Papa."

"Sal, the family is here gathered before our trip to the river, and we just wanted you to know that we are thinking of you and that I am carrying some stones on your behalf to the river," says his father.

Although this isn't as good as being home, Sal takes comfort knowing that he will be there in spirit and that his family is missing him as much as he is missing them.

"How are classes going, my son?" his father asks.

"Uh, fine," Sal replies.

He hates lying to his father—his classes aren't going well at all. There are days when he can't bring himself to get out of bed to go to class. He isn't sleeping at night, and he has lost his appetite. When he tries to study, he can't concentrate. All he can think of is what he thinks he heard John and Ayako say and what he thinks others are saying about him now.

He can't tell his father that he spends all of his time thinking about how much he has lost by moving away from home, his family, his friends, even his beloved pets. He isn't making any friends at college because of his isolation. He feels his life is meaningless and void of all beauty and joy, but he can't tell his father this.

They talk for a few more minutes. As they are winding up, Sal hears a knock at his door.

"Who is it?" Sal calls out.

"It's José from down the hall," comes the reply from the other side of the door.

"Dad," Sal says, "I've got to run. Have a wonderful day."

"We love you, Son."

José seems like a nice enough guy, but his culture is completely different from Sal's. José is studying dance, while Sal is studying finance. José is one of those guys who is always laughing and running up and down the hall in and out of rooms. No one dislikes José; Sal just hasn't connected with him.

"Sal, come on—open up. I know you're in there, and I'm not going away until you let me in," José insists.

Sal hears the determination in José's voice and gets up to answer the door. He remains standing firmly in the doorway, hoping José will get the idea and go away. He doesn't! Before Sal knows what has hit him, José is sprawled on his bed eating a bag of his chips and drinking one of his Cokes.

"What's up, Sal?" asks José.

"Nothing," replies Sal. He thinks there is no use opening up with José because he can't possibly understand the loneliness. "He is always surrounded by friends, and everyone likes him," Sal thinks.

"Come on, Sal," José says. "You've been moping around here for days. I'm really beginning to worry about you. I haven't seen you go to class in a week, and you are hardly leaving your room. You are not eating regularly, and it seems like you sleep 20 hours a day. If you don't want to talk to me, don't you think you should talk to someone?"

Case Study Analysis

Name _____ Date _____

Class _____ Section _____

1. What are the **facts** you KNOW about the case?

   _____

   _____

2. What are some **logical assumptions** you can make about the case?

   _____

   _____

   _____

   _____

3. What are the **problems** involved in the case as you see it?

   _____

   _____

   _____

4. What is the **root problem** (the main issue)?

   _____

   _____

5. What do you estimate is the **cause of the root problem**?

   _____

   _____

6. What are the **reasons** that the root problem exists?

   _____

   _____

   _____

7. What is (are) the **solution(s)** to the problem?

   _____

   _____

   _____

8. Are there any **moral and/or ethical considerations** to your solution?

_____

_____

9. What are the **consequences** of your solution?

_____

_____

_____

10. What are the **"real-world" implications** for this case?

_____

_____

_____

11. How will the **lives of the people in the case study be changed** because of your proposed solution?

_____

_____

_____

12. Where are some **areas on campus** that one could get help with the problems associated with this case?

_____

_____

13. Where are some **areas beyond the campus** that one could get help with the problems associated with this case?

_____

_____

_____

_____

_____

14. What **personal advice** would you give to Sal?

_____

_____

_____

I Love You to Death

"Oakdale Police Department, may I help you?"

"Yeah, this is campus security over at the college. We need an officer at Charlton Resident Hall."

"We have someone on the way, sir. They'll be there momentarily," the operator says.

Richard and Deborah meet in first-year orientation. They are randomly assigned together in an ice-breaking activity and later are seated together at a luncheon. It isn't love at first sight, but they both feel an attraction and an immediate chemistry between them. At the end of the day's activities, Richard asks Deborah if she is interested in a movie later in the week. She gladly accepts and is delighted that she has met someone so nice and friendly on the first day.

As the week moves on, Richard and Deborah call each other every night, and on Friday they agree to a movie and pizza afterward. They arrive back at the residence hall around 12:30 A.M. Politely, Richard walks Deborah to the door, kisses her, and asks if she would like to go to the campus lunch mixer on Saturday. She gladly agrees. They kiss again, and Richard turns to leave.

"Richard," Deborah says, "I had a great time. I'm already looking forward to tomorrow."

"I had a great time too," Richard says. "I'll pick you up at 11:00. Rest well."

Saturday rolls around. At 11:00, Richard and Deborah head to the center of campus for lunch, entertainment, and a street fair. They stroll through the grounds gathering free key chains, pens, and flyers from vendors. They have lunch, and sit on the grass listening to the band play. The weather is wonderful, and lunch is great. They sit and watch other students playing Frisbee and tossing footballs. To Deborah, this is just what college is supposed to be about. Everything feels right.

Later in the evening, they walk back to Deborah's room and she invites Richard in. They sit on her bed watching TV and talking about their pasts, their goals, and their dreams. Gently, Richard kisses Deborah, and she is receptive to his moves.

"I really like being with you," he says. "It's like we've known each other for years."

"I know," Deborah whispers. "This is very nice."

Over the course of the next few weeks, Deborah and Richard see more of each other. Deborah even changes her class schedule so that she and Richard are in the same Psychology class together. One day during Psychology, Professor Bennett divides the class into groups. Richard and Deborah are not in the same group. Richard's group consists of three males and two females. Deborah's group consists of two females and four males. As the groups meet, Professor Bennett asks that each group get to know other members of the group. To Deborah's surprise, one of the guys in her group is from her hometown. They had gone to different high schools but knew several acquaintances in common.

Toward the end of the class, each group seems to be progressing well with the task at hand, but Deborah's group is livelier than the others. They have had a good time, have gotten to know one another, and just seem to click together quite well. They have several good, hearty laughs as they work on the Psychology project. At the end of the class, Professor Bennett gives the assignment for the next meeting. Each group is to reassemble and complete their presentation to be given to the class.

After class, Richard makes several comments about Deborah's group. He seems jealous and somewhat angry that her group was laughing and having a good time.

"What was that all about in there?" he asks.

"What was *what* about?" Deborah questions him solemnly.

"That laughing and giggling with those guys."

"What guys, Richard?"

"Those guys in your group. All three of them were just touching you and patting you on the shoulder. Were you teasing them?"

"Richard, we were just getting to know one another. Mark is from Philly. He went to St. Mary's High," Deborah tries to explain.

"Oh, so you're real cozy with him now, are you?" Richard mocks.

"Richard, what's gotten into you?"

"*Me?*" Richard asks sternly. "I thought we had something going on here. I thought we were on to something. Then I see you flirting with every guy in the class."

"I was *not* flirting, Richard," Deborah states emphatically. "We were getting to know one another. I can't believe you're acting like this."

As they walk toward the residence hall, Richard informs Deborah that he does not want her to be in that group anymore. "You'll sit with our group on Wednesday."

"Richard, you can't tell me where to sit, and besides, I have a project to complete just like you do."

Richard grabs her arm and twists her around. "I'm telling you that I don't want you with those guys. You're making a fool of yourself—and of me."

Deborah is in shock over Richard's attitude and outbursts. "Let go of my arm, Richard. You're hurting me."

"And you're hurting me!" Richard yells.

Deborah forces her arm loose and begins to walk away. "Deborah, where are you going? We're supposed to go eat."

"You go alone, Richard," Deborah states firmly. "I don't want to see you right now."

She turns and walks briskly to the residence hall. She is numb over what has just happened. "Who was that?" she thinks. "Whackos, they're all whackos!"

Later that evening, she looks at her wrist to find that Richard grabbed her so forcefully that she is now bruised. She puts some ice on the area to keep it from swelling. When her roommate comes in, she notices the area and asks what happened. She tells her that she fell on the sidewalk and twisted her wrist.

"You need to see the nurse, girl," Emily says. "It could be broken."

"No!" Deborah says sternly. "I'll be just fine."

Later that evening, the phone rings. It is Richard. He tells Deborah that he is sorry for getting so mad.

"I just care about you so much, and seeing you with those guys made me very jealous," he says.

"Richard, there is no need to be jealous. We're in a group together, not an orgy."

"I know, I know," he says. "I just went crazy because I really want us to be together. Do you mind if I come over?"

"I'm already in the bed," Deborah tells him. "I'll see you tomorrow at breakfast."

Tuesday morning comes. Deborah opens her door to find Richard waiting with a bouquet of flowers. "I'm sorry," he tells her. She accepts the flowers, and they have breakfast.

Later that evening, Richard phones Deborah and asks if he can come over. Deborah tells him that she is studying and working on the Psychology project.

"I'll just see you in class tomorrow, and we can have lunch afterward if that is OK," she says.

"Are you sure I can't help you study?" Richard asks.

"I've got to get this done, and if you're here, we'll just watch TV or talk or . . . *no*, you can't come over," she says jokingly. "I'll see you tomorrow."

At 6:30 P.M., Deborah's Psychology group arrives to complete their project. All members are present. At 7:00, the doorbell rings and Deborah rises to answer the door. As she opens it, she is shocked to find Richard.

"What are you doing here?" she asks. "I told you I had to work on the Psychology project."

"Oh, I see what you're working on, baby. I see it now with both eyes," he says mockingly as he enters the room. "Is this why you didn't want me to come over?"

"Richard, you need to leave," she says.

Richard enters the room yelling as the study group stares at him.

"Oh, I plan to leave, but not before I show you and a few people here that I mean business about our relationship."

Case Study Analysis

Name _____ Date _____

Class _____ Section _____

1. What are the **facts** you KNOW about the case?

   _____

   _____

   _____

   _____

2. What are some **logical assumptions** you can make about the case?

   _____

   _____

   _____

   _____

3. What are the **problems** involved in the case as you see it?

   _____

   _____

   _____

   _____

4. What is the **root problem** (the main issue)?

   _____

5. What do you estimate is the **cause of the root problem**?

   _____

   _____

6. What are the **reasons** that the root problem exists?

   _____

   _____

   _____

7. What is (are) the **solution(s)** to the problem?

   _____

   _____

   _____

8. Are there any **moral and/or ethical considerations** to your solution?

_____

_____

_____

9. What are the **consequences** of your solution?

_____

_____

_____

10. What are the **"real-world" implications** for this case?

_____

_____

_____

11. How will the **lives** of the people in the case study **be changed** because of your proposed solution?

_____

_____

_____

12. Where are some **areas on campus** that one could get help with the problems associated with this case?

_____

_____

_____

13. Where are some **areas beyond the campus** that one could get help with the problems associated with this case?

_____

_____

_____

14. What **personal advice** would you give to Deborah?

_____

_____

_____

Sexual Behavior

Perhaps there is no other single aspect of human life more important than our intimate encounters with others. Our sexual behavior determines if we will be parents, if we will have—and pass along—sexually transmitted diseases, and if we will live to be 40 or 100. While our sexual behavior is our own responsibility, there may be others who try to encroach on our plans for intimacy.

4

CASE 1 It Was Only One Night

Jim and his classmates listen to a guest lecturer speak about HIV, AIDS, and other STDs only to learn that the speaker believes that a woman can give AIDS to a man through sex. Jim and his friends laugh at the idea and decide to bring up the topic for discussion in the next class. Surprised at the varied responses, Jim begins to worry about his own sexual behavior and how many times he might have put himself at risk.

CASE 2 That Wasn't Sex, Was It?

As a senior in high school, Victoria has been sexually active. At some time, she contracts a sexually transmitted disease, and though it is curable, it emotionally scars her. As a result, she decides to abstain from sex until she marries. This is not as easy as she thinks it will be. She is struggling with the pressures of her boyfriend and her girl-friends. She begins to question her own decisions.

CASE 3 Sex in the City?

Sylvia enters college as a first-year student after having worked for several years to save money while attending class at the local community college. She leaves her sheltered life in a small town to attend college in New York City, where she intends to pursue her dream. More mature because of her age and her work experience, she decides to capitalize on these advantages and start a practicum that will continue to add to her resume. Her major is art history, and her career goal is to become a curator at a large metropolitan museum. Although she is older and experienced, she is ill prepared for what awaits her on her practicum.

It Was Only One Night

"The guest lecturer in Dr. Callahan's class today was a joke," Jim says. "There is no way that a man can get AIDS from a woman." He indeed laughs it off as fiction to his friends Peru and Meg. Meg tells him that it *is* true, but her reasoning is muffled by the grunts, laughs, and groans from Jim and Peru.

"It's just crazy," Peru says. "Someone's bodily fluids have to be left, and a woman can't leave bodily fluid in a man." He laughs again. "It just ain't gonna happen."

"Yeah," Jim says. "It's about as crazy as saying that you can't get pregnant on your first time or if you do it standing up. We know that stuff isn't true."

"All right," Meg says, "keep on believing that a man can't get AIDS from a woman, and the last laugh will be on you."

Jim doesn't think too much more about the lecture or the conversation until later in the evening when he passes the gym on the way to his residence hall. Several guys are leaving the gym dribbling a basketball. He stops dead in his tracks. "Magic," he thinks. "How did Magic Johnson get AIDS?" He feels his face getting warmer and feels his knees weaken a little. "There has to be more to the story," he thinks. "Magic must have been doing something else."

Jim awakens in the middle of the night, and the lecture, Magic, Meg, and his past all haunt him. Jim realizes that he has slept with more than 10 women in the past year, many times without using any type of protection. In the back of his mind, he wonders about the reality of a man contracting AIDS from a woman. "Is it possible?" he wonders. He tries to sleep again, but sleep eludes him.

The next day, Jim wanders over to the library to review some reserve materials for his AutoCAD class. He can't keep his mind on designing a building when yesterday's lecture pounds in his brain. He goes over to the computer and enters a search for AIDS, which results in over 217,500 articles, book, tapes, and other media. He narrows the search by typing in "contracting AIDS." The results are still overwhelming.

As he begins to look over the articles and skim through hundreds of sites, he thinks about all that he knows about AIDS. "I know that a man can give it to another man and that a man can give it to a woman," he thinks. "Mothers can pass it to unborn children, and you can get it from sharing needles." His mind wanders for a moment. "I've just never heard much about straight men getting AIDS from women."

Jim pulls up a few articles on the Internet and as he reads, his mind goes in a thousand directions. "OK," he thinks, "I'm a straight guy, I don't do

drugs, and I use a condom sometimes. How much at risk could I be?" As he reads a few articles about contracting AIDS, he thinks, "This is just crazy. I'm worrying myself for nothing. The girls I've been with don't sleep around with many guys."

But in the back of his mind, Jim knows the truth. He knows that 3 of the 10 women with whom he has slept were strangers he met in a bar. "If they slept with me," he thinks, "maybe they have slept around with other guys. I don't know anything about them, and they don't know anything about me." Jim's fear level increases as he reads and thinks more. "Why did that professor invite that speaker to our class anyway? He's just causing grief," he thinks.

Jim, Meg, and Peru meet in front of the Science Building on Wednesday for the next class with Professor Callahan. The discussion on sexual behavior and personal responsibility continues, and Jim raises his hand.

"Doc," he asks, "do you believe what the speaker said yesterday about a man getting AIDS from a woman?"

The professor looks shocked, and quietness falls over the room.

"Howard Moore is one of the most respected AIDS educators in America, Jim. I trust his opinions and advice completely. He has been working with people with HIV and AIDS for over 18 years, and few people know more or have seen more with this epidemic than he has. So, yes, I do believe, well, I *know* that a man can get AIDS from a woman."

Dr. Callahan continues, "What do you all think? What is your opinion on the matter?" All is quiet for a moment, but then one student raises his hand and says, "Dr. Callahan, I've heard that HIV is not really what causes AIDS." Immediately, other class members began to speak.

"That's just crazy," says one student. "Don't you think that in 20 years, they'll know what causes AIDS now?"

"I think it was man-made to kill off some of the population," interjects another student.

"If you're abstinent, why worry about it at all?" another student asks forcefully.

Dr. Callahan realizes that he has his hands full with the varying viewpoints and surrounding controversy. "OK," he says, "Let's start at the beginning. Let's review what Mr. Moore said yesterday about what we know for sure about HIV and AIDS."

After the class is over, Jim is more worried than ever. He realizes that regardless of whether he knows his partners or not, he has put himself at some degree of risk by having multiple partners and not practicing safer sex all of the time.

At 1:55 P.M., Jim walks into the Mahoney Student Center and takes the elevator to the third floor. He gets off the elevator and walks toward the Student Health Center for his 2:00 appointment. His heart is beating fast, and he can barely catch his breath. As he reaches to open the door, he hesitates, catches his breath, and wonders whether he wants to know the answer.

Case Study Analysis

Name _____   Date _____

Class _____   Section _____

1. What are the **facts** you KNOW about the case?

_____

_____

_____

2. What are some **logical assumptions** you can make about the case?

_____

_____

_____

3. What are the **problems** involved in the case as you see it?

_____

_____

_____

4. What is the **root problem** (the main issue)?

_____

_____

5. What do you estimate is the **cause of the root problem**?

_____

_____

6. What are the **reasons** that the root problem exists?

_____

_____

_____

7. What is (are) the **solution(s)** to the problem?

_____

_____

_____

8. Are there any **moral and/or ethical considerations** to your solution?

_____

_____

_____

9. What are the **consequences** of your solution?

_____

_____

_____

10. What are the **"real-world" implications** for this case?

_____

_____

_____

11. How will the **lives** of the people in the case study **be changed** because of your proposed solution?

_____

_____

_____

12. Where are some **areas on campus** that one could get help with the problems associated with this case?

_____

_____

13. Where are some **areas beyond the campus** that one could get help with the problems associated with this case?

_____

_____

_____

14. What **personal advice** would you give to Jim?

_____

_____

That Wasn't Sex, Was It?

"Fredrico, please! We've discussed this time after time, and I'm getting tired of ending every date in an argument about sex!" Victoria says sternly.

"Come on, Vic, this is our fourth date! I thought things were clicking. I mean it's not like I'm some jerk trying to force myself on you. We've been going out together for a while, and we were in class together all last semester. I thought things were cool," replies Fredrico.

"And I thought you understood where I stand on the sex issue. I'm not having sex until I get married, Freddy—please don't press me on this," Victoria says.

"Hon, we're not talking about intercourse. We're talking about a little oral sex," Freddy replies. "No one considers that sex. I don't know how much longer I'm going to be able to go home to face a cold shower and my roommates talking about all the hot sex they are having. I mean Jim is giving me explicit details on every score he makes, and it's enough to drive me crazy—how much can you expect me to put up with?"

"I'm not asking you to go without it. Can't you take care of yourself?" asks Victoria.

"I can't believe you just suggested that. We're in college, not high school, and I was getting a whole lot more action in high school than I am here, so I'm out of here. If you ever decide that you're old enough to have a 'real' boyfriend, give me a call. I might be around, but then again I might not—I'm just not ready to deal with this sort of high school crap again. Later." Fredrico is gone.

The scene continues to play over and over in Vicki's mind for the next couple of days. Unfortunately, it is not the first time since she entered the university that this sort of thing has happened. In fact, Fredrico is the third boyfriend she has dealt with, and in truth, his exit has been the kindest one so far.

"I just don't get it," Victoria thinks. "Why is it that every boy I go out with wants sex and they want it right now?"

She asks this very question to some friends later that night over pizza. Sung Jung, her friend from English 101, says, "You know, I'm beginning to think that my school-work is the least of my worries here. I'm spending more time dealing with boyfriends and parties than I am with classes. My

71

roommate or one of our suitemates is always having a party out in the living room in hopes of finding a boyfriend. I never know who I'm going to find sleeping in our suite when I wake up!"

Brisa, her friend from biology class, says, "I don't know what the big deal is. I'm having the time of my life! I mean my parents told me they partied through college; that is, when they weren't having sit-ins or protesting this or that—man, those must have been the days. I'm just trying to keep my grades above passing. I'm going to live it up. I'm only in college once." This comment doesn't surprise Victoria, considering that the first time they met Brisa was wearing a T-shirt adorned with the quote "So many men, so little time."

"What do you think, Penelope?" asks Victoria. Penelope, who has been noticeably quiet throughout this discussion, finally says, "I know that you will all consider me incredibly old-fashioned, but I've never had sex and I don't intend to until I get married."

The entire group looks stunned. "Wait a minute. You and Alex have been going together for three years, and you haven't done *it?*" shrieks Brisa. This is overlapped by Sung Jung screaming "Oh my god, oh my god!"

"Alex and I are committed to God, and we believe in his commandment to not have sex out of marriage, so neither of us have, or will, until we get married next year," Penelope states.

That night as Victoria walks home, she thinks about everything that has taken place in the last 24 hours, and she can't help but think back to the most horrible day of her life. It was just over seven months ago. The day started with such joy and hope. Her mom wanted her to go see her gynecologist, before she went off to college, to have her first "pap smear" and exam. She also needed to get all of her shots updated to meet the university's medical requirements. Then they were going to go shopping for clothes and things for her residence hall room. She couldn't believe how excited she had been about starting this new chapter in her life.

That excitement hadn't lasted long. The first appointment of that memorable day had been with the gynecologist, who had started the appointment with some questions. Victoria had thought the questions were just too personal to answer, but when the doctor explained that she wasn't going to tell her mom, Victoria started talking to the doctor.

"Are you sexually active, Victoria?" Dr. Wilson asked.

"No, not really," answered Victoria.

"What do you mean 'not really'?" Dr. Wilson questioned.

"Well, you know, I've never done it."

"Done what, Victoria?"

"You know, had sex."

"Well, if you haven't had sex, what have you had?" asked Dr. Wilson.

"Well, I've given oral sex, but that's not really sex."

Dr. Wilson said, "Vic, I don't know who told you oral sex wasn't sex, but they were sadly misinformed. We need to have a serious conversation, but before we do that, let me examine you."

As she started the exam, she asked, "Have you had any problems with vaginal itching?"

"Well, yes, off and on, but I just figured that was because my cheerleading tights were rubbing me the wrong way after a game or tournament," replied Victoria.

"Have you ever experienced painful urination?" asked Dr. Wilson.

"Yes, about a year ago, but I took some of that over-the-counter stuff and after about 10 days it went away," replied Victoria.

"Is there something wrong, Doctor?" Victoria asked.

"Well, there seems to be evidence of a sexually transmitted disease, but I need to run a series of tests to make sure," replied Dr. Wilson.

"What?" Victoria screamed. "How can that be? I've never had sex!"

"I'm going to do this exam, Victoria, and then we need to have a serious conversation about sex and STDs and transmission," Dr. Wilson said sternly. "Your misconceptions might just cost you your life."

Victoria feels a wave of nausea rushing over her, even now, seven months later, as she recalls hearing those words. Chills run up and down Victoria's arms when she thinks about those days. Tears begin running down her face as she recalls the devastation in her mother's eyes when she told her she had contracted gonorrhea. It was during that painful experience that Victoria decides she was not going to have sex until she is much, much older—or even married. She also started reading articles about a movement called revirginizing. This relatively new movement described how women with previous sexual experience abstain from sex for extensive periods of time and then call themselves virgins again. It fit for her; Victoria was going to become a virgin again.

Seven months ago, that sounded great. "Three failed relationships, and all my friends are thinking I'm crazy," she thinks to herself. "It's been a long seven months. Am I overreacting?" Victoria wonders. "Is this revirginizing kick just a knee-jerk reaction from fear over a sexually transmitted disease? After all, everyone is having sex, and the guys are bailing on me fast," she tells herself.

While sitting in her residence hall pondering these questions, her phone rings. "Hello," Victoria says.

"Hi, Vic, it's Fredrico. Baby, I'm missing you so much."

"Fredrico, I miss you too," she says.

"Can I come over so we can talk about this thing?" he asks. She pauses, thinks for a moment, and answers, "Yes, you can, but don't think things haven't changed!"

"Things are always changing, baby. They always change," chants Fredrico.

Case Study Analysis

Name _____ Date _____

Class _____ Section _____

1. What are the **facts** you KNOW about the case?

   _____

   _____

   _____

2. What are some **logical assumptions** you can make about the case?

   _____

   _____

   _____

3. What are the **problems** involved in the case as you see it?

   _____

   _____

   _____

4. What is the **root problem** (the main issue)?

   _____

   _____

5. What do you estimate is the **cause of the root problem**?

   _____

   _____

6. What are the **reasons** that the root problem exists?

   _____

   _____

   _____

7. What is (are) the **solution(s)** to the problem?

   _____

   _____

   _____

8. Are there any **moral and/or ethical considerations** to your solution?

9. What are the **consequences** of your solution?

10. What are the **"real-world" implications** for this case?

11. How will the **lives** of the people in the case study **be changed** because of your proposed solution?

12. Where are some **areas on campus** that one could get help with the problems associated with this case?

13. Where are some **areas beyond the campus** that one could get help with the problems associated with this case?

14. What **personal advice** would you give to Victoria?

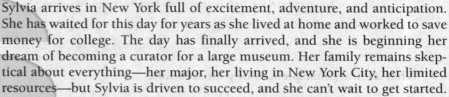

CASE 3   Sex in the City?

Sylvia arrives in New York full of excitement, adventure, and anticipation. She has waited for this day for years as she lived at home and worked to save money for college. The day has finally arrived, and she is beginning her dream of becoming a curator for a large museum. Her family remains skeptical about everything—her major, her living in New York City, her limited resources—but Sylvia is driven to succeed, and she can't wait to get started.

Although Sylvia worked as a waitress to save money, she volunteered to work with her art history professor at the local community college. While this job didn't offer her any compensation, the knowledge she gained from Mrs. Madden made it worth her time. Mrs. Madden, who became a professor after having worked as a curator in a large museum, understood Sylvia's desire to follow in her footsteps. She took extra time to coach and advise Sylvia and was excited to see her take the next step toward her goal. Impressed with Sylvia's desire to succeed and her love of art and sculpture, Mrs. Madden contacted one of her former colleagues at the New York Metropolitan Museum of Art.

When Sylvia comes in from class after having been in New York for only two weeks, she is thrilled to have a message from Mrs. Madden. Her mentor is always encouraging, and Sylvia needs a boost from someone who understands her struggles. Mrs. Madden informs Sylvia that she has spoken with her friend Francis Conway at the museum. Her message instructs Sylvia to call Mr. Conway the next day to arrange an interview. Mr. Conway has an opening for a practicum intern. Not only is this an excellent career opportunity, it is a paying job! And she can certainly use that!

Sylvia calls Mr. Conway between classes and arranges an interview for the next afternoon. She dresses carefully, selecting a simple black dress and understated jewelry. She takes the subway to her interview. Mr. Conway, a distinguished man in his fifties, is pleasant and encouraging and appears to be impressed with her knowledge and ambition. After walking her through the museum, he leads her back to his office. Sylvia is very pleased when Mr. Conway offers her the job as his personal intern. He reaches over and pats her knee in a fatherly fashion. Although this makes Sylvia a little uncomfortable, he is Mrs. Madden's friend after all. He tells her to report to work on Monday and that they will work out her schedule at that time.

Excited and eager to learn and to begin work, Sylvia arrives early on Monday and goes straight to Mr. Conway's office. He is not in, but she meets Jonathon, a senior intern, who has been instructed by Mr. Conway to show her the ropes and to get her started on a project. He tells her that he had worked closely with Mr. Conway's last intern, who left suddenly last semester.

All that week, Sylvia arrives early and works with Jonathon. She begins to feel comfortable and very fortunate to have this opportunity, to be able to learn from Mr. Conway, and to have Jonathon to advise her. After work on Friday, Jonathon suggests they have dinner. Sylvia accepts, and they leave for dinner. After the entrée arrives, Jonathon quizzes her about how she got the job and what she knows about Mr. Conway. While he alludes to problems with the last intern, he doesn't talk about specifics and she doesn't feel comfortable asking too many questions.

Sylvia arrives at work on Monday and is excited to find that Mr. Conway has returned from his business trip. He comes across the room, takes her coat, and kisses her cheek. Mr. Conway informs Sylvia that she will be working with him for the remainder of the week. They begin cataloging several new pieces of art that have arrived from Greece for an important show scheduled later during the month. Several times during the week, Mr. Conway brushes against her and once he reaches over her shoulder to pick up some notes and appears to linger longer than necessary. She wonders if it is just her imagination or does he seem to be "out of line" with his closeness. His "hello greeting" kisses on the cheek are now accompanied by an embracing hug that seems longer than necessary and not so fatherly as in the beginning. Mr. Conway now makes her feel uncomfortable. She wishes she had someone to discuss this situation with, but she doesn't feel that she can go to Mrs. Madden. After all, this is Mrs. Madden's friend, and what would she say to her? "What will Jonathon think if I mention this to him?" she thinks.

Sylvia doesn't see Jonathon that week, but on Monday he tells her that she is to work with him. Mr. Conway is out of town on another business trip. Jonathon comments on the fact that she doesn't seem herself. He inquires about Mr. Conway and how things are working out.

"They're fine, I guess," she says solemnly. Sylvia is evasive and changes the subject.

"Should I tell Jonathon about Mr. Conway's actions?" she wonders privately. "What will I tell him? Maybe this is all in my imagination. What if I'm wrong? What will Mrs. Madden think? Is this my fault?" The questions swirl in Sylvia's mind.

Mr. Conway returns on Wednesday from his business trip, walks in the office, and immediately goes over to Sylvia and hugs her and kisses her on the cheek. They begin work on the exhibit. He asks her if she will work late because he wants to get this project completed. Sylvia agrees, and he instructs her to order in food for the evening.

They take the food to his conference room, which is isolated from the rest of the building. All of this makes Sylvia very uncomfortable. She sits down and begins to put food on her plate. Suddenly, Mr. Conway closes the conference room door, moves behind her, and begins massaging her shoulders. He leans down and kisses the back of her neck in a very suggestive manner.

"We could be here all night," he says. "Just the two of us."

Case Study Analysis

Name _____   Date _____

Class _____   Section _____

1. What are the **facts** you KNOW about the case?

_____

_____

_____

2. What are some **logical assumptions** you can make about the case?

_____

_____

_____

3. What are the **problems** involved in the case as you see it?

_____

_____

_____

4. What is the **root problem** (the main issue)?

_____

_____

5. What do you estimate is the **cause of the root problem**?

_____

_____

6. What are the **reasons** that the root problem exists?

_____

_____

7. What is (are) the **solution(s)** to the problem?

_____

_____

8. Are there any **moral and/or ethical considerations** to your solution?

_____

_____

_____

9. What are the **consequences** of your solution?

_____

_____

_____

10. What are the **"real-world" implications** for this case?

_____

_____

_____

11. How will the **lives** of the people in the case study **be changed** because of your proposed solution?

_____

_____

_____

12. Where are some **areas on campus** that one could get help with the problems associated with this case?

_____

_____

_____

13. Where are some **areas beyond the campus** that one could get help with the problems associated with this case?

_____

_____

_____

14. What **personal advice** would you give to Sylvia?

_____

_____

_____

CHAPTER 5

Diversity

It has been said that our acceptance of diversity in the world is the true
acceptance of ourselves. Perhaps one of the most important lessons that
we can carry forth is the fact that humans have never been in
the world alone and they never will be. We are all a part of one
another, and only the truly educated understand the complexity
of this issue.

5

At a Glance

CASE 1   A World Away

Robert is attending a large university in North Carolina. He has always lived in the South and feels that he needs to stay in an environment to which he is accustomed. He has given no thought to the fact that a large university will include students from all over the country as well as the world. He is in for a culture shock as he arrives on campus.

CASE 2   Not an Ace in the Hole

Hugh is excited about his internship at Ace Chemicals. He is making great money, is learning about engineering, and has met a great coworker who helps him on a daily basis. Hugh's boss, however, is not as excited about Hugh's friendship with the coworker and warns him to stay away or suffer the consequences. Hugh is torn between an internship he loves and great money, or doing what he feels is right.

CASE 3   Kwanzaa Who?

A group of students enter the student center to find a new display about the African holiday tradition of Kwanzaa. After discussing the display, Varawon lets it be known that he feels the holiday is a crazy, made-up event to separate people even more than they already are. Varawon and his friends then encounter the students who created the display. An interesting and frightening conversation ensues.

A World Away

Robert has planned his college career carefully. He has chosen a university with an excellent reputation only two hours from his home so he can return often to visit family and friends. The school has an excellent reputation in Public Health, the major he plans to study. He has lots of friends from home on campus, so he feels comfortable almost immediately. His girlfriend, Kristen, has also selected the same university.

Basically, Robert has succeeded very well in transporting his network of friends to school with him. He sees very little need to branch out and meet new people. "Why bother?" he thinks. "I have a great group of friends, and things are going well."

Things go along smoothly for Robert. His grades are good, he and his friends from home have pledged a fraternity, and he has Kristen with him—all is well with his world. Little does he know that his carefully constructed little world is about to be turned upside down.

Tuesday afternoon is lab day for Robert's Biology class. His professor assigns new partners for each assignment. Today Robert arrives at his assigned station to find a strange-looking young woman who is covered from head to toe in what Robert later learns is required dress for Muslim women. Her head is covered in a *knumur*. Her dress is loose so as not to show the shape of her body, and the fabric is thick so the color of her skin is hidden. Only her face and hands are showing. Robert knows nothing about the Muslim culture. He can't imagine Kristen wearing anything like this. Anyway, after the September 11 tragedy, he is not interested in having anything to do with Arabs. "The whole bunch of them are just fanatics," he thinks.

Robert feels awkward, but what the heck—this is only one afternoon in his life, so he tries to make the best of it. He introduces himself—"Hi, my name is Robert Carpenter"—and offers his hand. The young woman does not look directly at him and does not shake his hand. Rather, she lowers her eyes and tells him that her name is Fareeha. She seems to be uncomfortable around American men, and he thinks she looks sad. "What does *Fareeha* mean?" he inquires. "It means joyful, happy," she replies. To himself Robert thinks, "You could have fooled me."

As they work on their assignment, Robert discovers that Fareeha is very bright. Obviously, she already knows everything about this assignment. As they work, he quizzes her about her background. He discovers that her family moved to North Carolina, where her father owns a very successful engineering firm. She, along with her brothers and sisters, are all studying engineering. Her family's expectations of her and her siblings are very demanding. She has to make A's or suffer her father's wrath. "So you must really love science and math?" Robert asks. "Actually, I don't," says Fareeha, "but I really have no choice. My father will not allow me to study anything but engineering. I would love to study music." Robert discovers that Fareeha is an excellent musician and practices the violin for hours daily. Apparently, she is allowed no outside social life. He wonders if her family will choose her husband.

Robert feels sorry for her and walks with her outside after class. He notices that other students look at them with contempt. He wonders if Fareeha faces this kind of behavior every day. He wants to tell them that she is really OK, that she's not from a terrorist family, but he doesn't know how to change people's prejudices. Robert is learning from this experience that people should be judged as individuals, not collectively.

Without realizing it, Robert has become interested in this girl and her strange culture. "Would you like to get something to drink?" he asks her shyly.

"I can't," she replies nervously. "My brother is picking me up in a few minutes."

Robert asks, "Could I meet him?"

"No," she says quickly and definitely. "I don't think that would be a good idea."

At that moment, her brother drives up and Fareeha runs to the car and leaves. He notices that her brother stares at him for a long time.

Robert can't get this different young woman off his mind. That night he begs off from going to the library and instead searches on the Internet for information about the Muslim culture. He reads an article about Muslim schools and is shocked to see what Fareeha has been required to practice. He studies Muslim family life and their customs. Fareeha has no choice but to wear that heavy, hot dress! As a believer in the Muslim religion, she has been taught to differentiate her dress from nonbelievers. The Prophet Pbuh stated, "Whoever wears a dress of fame in this world, Allah will clothe him with a dress of humiliation in the day of resurrection, then set it afire."

Robert looks for Fareeha at his next Biology class and goes to sit beside her. He tries to engage her in conversation, and she gradually begins to talk to him as the days go by. At every class period, Robert seeks her out and sits with her. He notices the rude stares and remarks, but he ignores them. More and more, Robert begins to look forward to seeing her and to learning about her customs, culture, and religion. He studies the Qur'an and Muhammad's teachings. While he finds them strange, he understands Fareeha better. Now that he knows her and has learned more about her family, he realizes that all Arabs are not terrorists.

Robert begins to admire Fareeha's discipline and faith. He learns that her religion teaches patience, humility, charity, fasting, and praise for Allah. He spends more and more time studying about her religion and culture. He attends her worship services and watches her family across the room. Robert is moving more and more away from his old friends, even Kristen, as he becomes more attracted to Fareeha.

"What in the world will my family think?" he wonders. "They think people from New York are foreigners. They'll never understand this. Me—interested in a Muslim woman, how can I ever explain this?"

Later in the evening, Kristen calls and reminds him that they are supposed to got to a movie that evening.

"I don't think I can go," Robert says apologetically.

"Why not?" Kristen asks.

"I'm just not feeling well tonight," he replies.

"Come on, Robert, this is the third time you've canceled a date in the past two weeks. What's going on?"

Case Study Analysis

Name _____   Date _____

Class _____   Section _____

1. What are the **facts** you KNOW about the case?

_____

_____

_____

2. What are some **logical assumptions** you can make about the case?

_____

_____

_____

3. What are the **problems** involved in the case as you see it?

_____

_____

_____

4. What is the **root problem** (the main issue)?

_____

_____

5. What do you estimate is the **cause of the root problem**?

_____

_____

6. What are the **reasons** that the root problem exists?

_____

_____

_____

7. What is (are) the **solution(s)** to the problem?

_____

_____

_____

8. Are there any **moral and/or ethical considerations** to your solution?

_____

_____

9. What are the **consequences** of your solution?

_____

_____

10. What are the **"real-world" implications** for this case?

_____

_____

_____

11. How will the **lives of the people** in the case study **be changed** because of your proposed solution?

_____

_____

_____

12. Where are some **areas on campus** that one could get help with the problems associated with this case?

_____

_____

_____

13. Where are some **areas beyond the campus** that one could get help with the problems associated with this case?

_____

_____

_____

14. What **personal advice** would you give to Robert?

_____

_____

_____

Not an Ace in the Hole

Hugh is excited beyond words about his internship at Ace Chemicals. His dream is to become a chemical engineer, and this internship is a giant step in that direction. His advisor in the Engineering Program, Ms. Hawkins, arranged the internship and worked with the supervisor to set up the schedule and details of the six-month project.

Hugh takes classes on Monday, Wednesday, and Friday and works at Ace on Tuesday and Thursday. In addition to getting experience with the internship, he is getting paid $15.50 per hour for his work. The deal is sweet, and he realizes how fortunate he is to have the opportunity.

Things are going well, and Hugh loves working with people who have the job he wants after graduation. Part of the internship requirement is that his immediate supervisor provides a monthly evaluation of his performance. At the end of the first month, Hugh's evaluation is sterling. His supervisor, Marvin Jones, raves about the quality of his work, his ability to learn things quickly, and his collegial attitude toward coworkers. Hugh is delighted, as is his advisor.

Shortly into the second month of his internship, Mr. Jones asks to speak with Hugh at 4:00 P.M. in his office. Hugh is worried since this is the first time Mr. Jones has asked to speak with him privately. In the back of his mind, however, he hopes that Mr. Jones is going to offer him a full-time job after graduation. "How sweet would that be?" he asks himself. "A built-in job."

At 4:00, Hugh enters Mr. Jones's office and takes a seat. "Hugh," Mr. Jones begins, "your work is great, son. We've had many interns here, and I'd say that you're at the top of the list when it comes to performance." Hugh can't help but smile. "Thank you, Mr. Jones," he says. "I love my work here. It's what I want to do for a living."

"How are your classes going?" Mr. Jones asks.

"They're great," says Hugh. "I have a 3.8 GPA."

"That is very impressive," Mr. Jones comments. "You've a lot going for you, and the reason I called you in today is to give you some advice."

Hugh can feel his heart beating faster. He is excited and very happy that Mr. Jones is pleased with his work.

"Hugh, several people on the floor have told me that they see you eating lunch with Paul Konik."

"Yes, sir," says Hugh. "I do almost every day that I am here. He seems to be a great guy, and he's really helped me with several projects."

"Hugh, I don't know how to say this except bluntly. Mr. Konik will not be with us very much longer. You don't need to be associating with him or seen with him."

"What did he do, Mr. Jones?" Hugh asks.

"Well," says Mr. Jones, "let's just say that he's not 'one of us.'"

"'One of us'?" Hugh questions. "What does that mean?"

"Come on, boy," quips Mr. Jones in a sharp tone. "Do I have to put it into direct words for you?"

"Yes, sir, I think you do," says Hugh. "He works hard, is very bright, and has helped me greatly since I began my internship."

"Well, the reason he helps you is because he probably wants to sleep with you, boy. Haven't you noticed that he's a queer?"

"Mr. Jones, Paul told me about his sexual orientation the first day I met him. He told me about his partner and their daughter," Hugh informs him.

"And you choose to sit with him and be seen with him? Boy, you've got a lot to learn about the real world of work."

"Sir, I don't mean to be rude or disrespect you, but I consider Paul to be a good friend and a trusted colleague. I won't stop sitting with him because he's gay. He is a good man and a hard worker," Hugh says.

"Well, you need to listen to me and take my advice, son. You have nothing to gain from being seen with him. It could seriously damage your internship, your evaluations, and any prospect for future employment," Mr. Jones states.

"I just don't understand sir, I . . ." Hugh is cut off by Mr. Jones.

"The only thing for you to understand is this—you hang around with queers and people will think you're a queer. We don't tolerate that kind of sickness around here. I can't make you do nothing, the choice is yours, but be warned. Your future with Ace is in jeopardy."

Hugh leaves the office stunned. He can't believe that he heard the conversation that just took place. "How can this happen in the 21st century?" he thinks. "Jeez, I feel like I've gone back to the dark ages." Hugh likes Paul but is torn between a future with Ace and doing what he feels is right. He certainly can't afford to lose his $15.50-an-hour job in the middle of the semester. He knows what to do, but the threats of isolation and rejection are overwhelming. For the first time in almost two months, Hugh dreads for Thursday to roll around.

On Thursday, Hugh enters the plant with hesitation and frustration. "Crap," he thinks to himself. "You might know the first person I see is Mr. Jones."

"Morning, Hugh," Mr. Jones shouts. "How's the world?"

"Good morning, Mr. Jones," Hugh says softly. He can't believe that Mr. Jones is acting like nothing has happened. "How two-faced can you be?" he wonders.

Lunchtime comes, and Hugh is torn. He even considers taking a later lunch so that he does not have to make a decision about where to sit. "It is going to be very obvious that something is wrong if I don't sit with Paul," he thinks. "But, I don't need any more lectures from Mr. Jones."

Hugh walks into the canteen, where Paul is already seated in a booth in the corner. He makes eye contact, and Paul waves him over.

"Have you had a good week so far?" Paul asks.

"It's been weird, Paul. Unlike any other."

"What's the deal, buddy? Can I help?"

Hugh decides to sit down and talk to Paul about what happened. "Paul," he begins, "Mr. Jones called me in yesterday and asked me . . . no, he told me in so many words . . . that I should not sit with you or be seen with you if I wanted to have a career here. He also told me that he is planning to let you go."

"Jeez," Paul begins, "he's hated me since he found out I'm gay. He's tried to fire me three times this year. He's just an air bag who hates anyone different from him and his cronies."

"But aren't you worried about him and what he can do to you?" Hugh asks.

"Yes, but I can't let that rule my life. I do my job, I do it well, and I let that speak for me. I don't bother anyone, and I don't push anything on anyone. It is their problem."

"Yes, but . . ."

"Don't worry, Hugh, there are always going to be bigots and people who have prejudices. It's just a fact of life."

They finish their lunch, and as Hugh and Paul leave, he notices several men in another part of the canteen looking at them, whispering, and then a hearty laugh erupts. Hugh can feel his temper rising.

After work, Hugh walks through the parking lot toward his car. As he approaches the car, he sees a piece of white paper tucked under the windshield wiper blade. He looks around the lot to see if he sees anyone else or to see if other cars have notes on them. He sees nothing. He takes the note from the car. It contains one word in huge letters, "FAGGOT."

Case Study Analysis

Name _____ Date _____

Class _____ Section _____

1. What are the **facts** you KNOW about the case?

   _____
   _____
   _____

2. What are some **logical assumptions** you can make about the case?

   _____
   _____
   _____

3. What are the **problems** involved in the case as you see it?

   _____
   _____
   _____

4. What is the **root problem** (the main issue)?

   _____

5. What do you estimate is the **cause of the root problem**?

   _____
   _____

6. What are the **reasons** that the root problem exists?

   _____
   _____
   _____

7. What is (are) the **solution(s)** to the problem?

   _____
   _____
   _____

8. Are there any **moral and/or ethical considerations** to your solution?

_____

_____

_____

9. What are the **consequences** of your solution?

_____

_____

_____

10. What are the **"real-world" implications** for this case?

_____

_____

_____

11. How will the **lives** of the people in the case study **be changed** because of your proposed solution?

_____

_____

_____

12. Where are some **areas on campus** that one could get help with the problems associated with this case?

_____

_____

_____

13. Where are some **areas beyond the campus** that one could get help with the problems associated with this case?

_____

_____

_____

14. What **personal advice** would you give to Hugh?

_____

_____

_____

Kwanzaa Who?

Circe, Tara, and Varawon leave their sociology class and decide to have lunch in the student center before going to the library to complete their group project. Upon entering the student center, they see a group of people working on one of the 15 large display cases reserved for clubs and special occasions. The students are placing colorful garments in the case and having a joyful time as they listen to music and laugh with one another.

After they finish their lunch, Circe, Tara, and Varawon walk past the display case and see that it has been designated for Kwanzaa. In the case are brightly colored fabrics, candles, books, African artifacts, and fruit. There are also placards explaining what each item means and describing the holiday of Kwanzaa.

"Wow," Tara says. "That's colorful. They put a lot of work into that display."

"It's so stupid," Varawon says. "It's a made-up holiday that means nothing to most of the people in America or anywhere else."

"Don't hold back now," Circe says. "Let us know exactly how you feel."

"I *feel* like it is just another way to separate us all. Why do blacks, oops, I'm sorry, African-Americans, have to have a separate Christmas? Why can't they just enjoy what everyone else enjoys?"

"Don't you think that all holidays are made up?" Tara asks.

"Yes, they are to some extent, but at least they have some degree of history behind them. Kwanzaa wasn't even thought of until 1966," Varawon says.

"Why are you so angry about a display case?" Tara asks.

"Because it just shows us that we can't even get along well enough to have the same holidays," Varawon answers. "Look at the placards in there: Kwanzaa, Nguzo Saba, Ujamaa, Imani . . . you can't even pronounce that crap. How can you celebrate something that you can't even pronounce?"

"Just because you can't pronounce it," Circe says, "doesn't mean that others can't."

"Yeah," Tara says. "That's the reason for the display . . . to help educate us on another cultural tradition."

"Well, I say it's a waste of space, and I don't think that the university should be supporting separatism."

Just as they are about to walk off from the display, Darren and Bianca approach them. "Do you have any questions about the display or about Kwanzaa?" Darren asks.

"No," says Varawon.

"He thinks it's stupid," Tara reports to Darren and Bianca. "Tell them how stupid the display is, Varawon."

"I did not say it was stupid," he disagrees. "I said it promotes separatism and drives a wedge further between the races."

"No, sir," says Circe. "You said it was stupid."

"Alright, yes, I think it is stupid to make up a holiday and think that everyone is going to fall over to celebrate it," Varawon says.

"Well," Bianca says, "the reason we put the display up is so that we could try to educate the student body about Kwanzaa and the ancient cultures of Africa. Did you know that Kwanzaa is a Swahili word that means, 'first fruits'?"

"Yes," Darren adds, "and Kwanzaa has been celebrated in Africa as far back as ancient Egyptian times. It is a celebration of the common bonds of people, a time for thanks, and a jubilant celebration of the good things about family, community, culture, and the good things about existence itself."

"Sounds like Thanksgiving to me," Varawon says. "Why can't you celebrate all of that at Thanksgiving with the rest of America?"

"Kwanzaa is more than thanksgiving," Bianca answers. "It is about unity, self-determination, collectivity, economics, purpose, creativity, and faith celebrated by millions throughout the world."

As the discussion continues, Varawon asks, "Why can't you try to see it from our perspective? Why can't you understand that a holiday less than 40 years old sounds like hogwash to almost everyone? I just see it as blacks trying to separate themselves even more from mainstream society."

"We just don't see it that way," Darren explains. "White people celebrate Kwanzaa too."

"Look at this placard right here. . . . Read that card right there," Varawon points to the display case. "'*You cannot mix Kwanzaa holiday or its practice with any other culture.*' You see, right there—separation. Christmas is for everyone. Thanksgiving is for everyone, and Kwanzaa is not. It just separates us all."

"Varawon," Tara asks, "Do you feel the same way about Chanukah? Do you think that it is a crazy, made-up holiday that separates us all too?"

"Not as much as this one, but yes, Chanukah is nothing but separatism too. Why can't Jews celebrate holidays with everyone else?"

"Mainly because their religion is different from ours and they value customs and traditions that are not a part of the Christian faith," Circe says.

"And," Bianca adds, "Chanukah is much older than Christmas and has its roots in the Bible just as Christmas does."

"I'm just trying to say that we have so much that separates us by birth, why create another thing that causes us to be different? Why can't you understand that?" Varawon pleads.

"Let me extend my hand to you and say that we would love to have you come celebrate Kwanzaa with us just one time, and you will understand that this is about creating community, not destroying it," Darren says as he extends his hand.

"I would love to see you three too," Bianca adds. "Take your time and enjoy the display," she says as she and Darren walk away.

"Just crap," Varawon says. "Pure crap."

"How can you say that, never having experienced a Kwanzaa celebration, never having read or studied Kwanzaa, and never having talked to people who know more than you about the issue?" Circe asks Varawon. "I thought you were more open-minded than this."

"I'm one of the most open-minded people you know," Varawon says. "I just don't agree with what Kwanzaa is about. Can't we just agree to disagree?"

"I guess we'll have to," Tara says. "Are you going to take them up on their offer to join the Kwanzaa celebration?"

"You'll see me at Kwanzaa when I see them put up a Christmas tree and sing 'Silent Night.'"

Case Study Analysis

Name _____ Date _____

Class _____ Section _____

1. What are the **facts** you KNOW about the case?

_____

_____

2. What are some **logical assumptions** you can make about the case?

_____

_____

_____

3. What are the **problems** involved in the case as you see it?

_____

_____

_____

4. What is the **root problem** (the main issue)?

_____

_____

5. What do you estimate is the **cause of the root problem**?

_____

_____

6. What are the **reasons** that the root problem exists?

_____

_____

_____

7. What is (are) the **solution(s)** to the problem?

_____

_____

_____

8. Are there any **moral and/or ethical considerations** to your solution?

_____

_____

_____

9. What are the **consequences** of your solution?

_____

_____

_____

10. What are the **"real-world" implications** for this case?

_____

_____

_____

11. How will the **lives** of the people in the case study **be changed** because of your proposed solution?

_____

_____

_____

12. Where are some **areas on campus** that one could get help with the problems associated with this case?

_____

_____

_____

13. Where are some **areas beyond the campus** that one could get help with the problems associated with this case?

_____

_____

_____

14. What **personal advice** would you give to Varawon?

_____

_____

_____

Academic Success

AT A GLANCE

College life is about new encounters, personal growth, experiences of a life-time, entertainment, enrichment, and, yes, learning. Often, first-year students focus on issues beyond the classroom with more fervor than issues related to academic success. Understanding how you learn, how to take notes, how to study, how to take tests, and how to think more critically and creatively will ensure your ability to continue your encounters beyond the classroom.

6

At a Glance

CASE 1 Poetry in Motion

Melodie and Todd are enrolled in the same poetry class. Melodie is an English major, and Todd is a Music major. The professor has a rather unorthodox way of teaching the class. Todd loves the interactive nature of interpretation, while Melodie wishes the professor would just tell them what the poetry means and move on. Who will succeed?

CASE 2 This Is a Test, This Is Only a Test

Calista has trouble taking tests. She makes it through high school because she is very good at group work, projects, and writing, but she has immense fear and anxiety when she takes a test. Her college history professor gives only two tests for the entire semester. She is worried that her grades will suffer because two tests make up the entire grade for the class. Can she make it?

CASE 3 His Cheatin' Heart

Sonny and Niles are friends taking classes together at Our Lady of the Pines College. The college has a very strict honor code that prohibits students from cheating, plagiarizing, or acting in inappropriate ways. The policy also states that students can be removed from the college if they see an act of dishonesty and don't report it. Something happens between Sonny and Niles that will put the honor code—and their friendship—to the test.

Poetry in Motion

Melodie and Todd are enrolled in English 227, Introduction to Poetry. They both enroll in the class because of their desire to learn more about poetry. Todd is a music major, and Melodie is an English major. Specifically, Melodie is taking the course because she has trouble understanding poetry and because it is a required course. Todd is enrolled in the course because he thinks that it will help him write better lyrics to his songs.

Shortly after the semester begins, Professor North assigns a poem from the text. He instructs the class that each student will present her interpretation of the poem to the class. "This is the first of many presentations you will have this semester," he states. "Interpretation and poetry cannot be separated. Yes, I'm also a believer in oral interpretation. . . . I want to hear what you think."

The first poem is a brief work, but one that is packed with deep meaning and symbolism. Todd works hard on the poem and tries to figure out what the poet is really trying to say. Melodie works hard on her interpretation also. The next day, members of the small class begin to deliver what they feel is the essence of the poem.

"I think that she is trying to say that human nature is learned," narrates Simpson, another English major in the class.

"Well, I read this thing about 187 times, and I don't have a clue about what she's getting at," says Willard jokingly. "Seriously, I think she's talking about her love of nature." The class laughs because Willard has made it known that he is in the class because it is the *only* upper-level English course that would fit with his work schedule.

"Melodie," Dr. Rundell says. "Let's hear from you."

Cautiously, Melodie approaches the lectern and begins. "I think that the line 'the loblolly pines stood in rows like toy soldiers' is really about how we see one another," she says. When she finishes her interpretation, the professor calls on Todd. Todd approaches the podium and begins. "I really loved this poem because I felt like she was talking to me, talking about my life. I feel that she is trying to say that when death comes, the world does not die, the planets don't misalign, and the trees don't stop growing. Just because we die, our environment does not."

"Well," says the professor. "We do have some work to do here. Willard, she is not talking about trees. Simpson, I don't think she was talking specifically about human nature either. Melodie, I don't mean to be discouraging, but you were way off base. Todd, I'm glad you enjoyed the poem, and I'm glad that someone got it." Todd beamed with delight, while the other students sat there feeling odd and somewhat inadequate.

"Todd," the professor begins, "how did you come up with the metaphor of death?"

"Well, sir," Todd says, "I read it a few times, and then I just put it away for a day. Then I came back to it and read it again. I thought I knew what she was getting at, but I decided to read it again with some music in the background. That really helped me. I know it sounds funny, but it wasn't until I read the poem with the music in the background that I finally understood what she meant. That music took me to a place where I needed to be to understand that poem."

After class, Melodie and Willard approach Todd and rag him about being the "teacher's pet." "Oh, I believe that she was talking about death," they tease. "Oh, and yes, Professor, I find that listening to the London Philharmonic assists me in the overall interpretation of the lyric piece," Willard continues.

"You're just jealous because I got it," Todd says jokingly.

"Yeah," says Melodie, "I *am*. And I'm nervous over this piece we've got to read for Monday. How are we going to find a picture that is representative of this poem when we don't even understand the poem?" she asks.

"Oh, leave it to Todd," Willard jokes. "He'll show up with an original oil painting on loan from the Louvre." They all laugh as they go their separate ways, but in her heart, Melodie knows that she has never had much luck at understanding or interpreting poetry. She knows that she has her work cut out for her with this homework assignment. "I have to get this one," she thinks. "I have got to understand it, and I've got to find a picture that helps bring it to life."

Over the weekend, she works hard to understand the poem. She reads it often, and yes, even listens to a piece of classical music that she loves while reading it. She takes Todd's advice and puts the poem away for a day and comes back to it on Sunday. After lunch on Sunday, she strolls over to the local bookstore to flip through magazines to see if she can find a picture that she thinks represents the poem.

When Monday rolls around, she enters the class with her picture only to find Todd, Willard, Simpson, and a few others already talking about the poem. They have a variety of pictures, and none seems to match what she brought. "Oh, good," she thinks. "I'll be the fool again."

The professor enters the room with a folder of pictures and a roll of masking tape. "OK," he begins, "I'd like for you to take a piece of tape and post your interpretative picture on the wall. Then we'll walk around in silence, review the pictures, and talk about who brought what and why." They all take strips of tape and post their pictures. The professor gives the class about 10 minutes to walk around and look at the displays. He then calls time.

"OK," he says, "let's talk about these. I want you to take a card and write down on the card the picture that you feel best represents the poem . . . *excluding* your own." After this is done, he tallies the vote and walks over to the winning picture. "Who brought this?" he asks. Embarrassed but quietly proud, Todd raises his hand. "I did, sir." The class moans and begins to joke with Todd again about his interpretative nature. Once again, Todd has, in the professor's mind, understood the assignment and earned his praise.

After class, Todd once again bears the brunt of jokes outside the classroom. Melodie, however, isn't as jovial. "I don't understand why we can't just read the poem and have him talk about it. I'd understand it that way. I want to hear what *he* has to say about the poems. Why does he have to make everything so hard? Why do we have to be so 'creative' with stupid poetry?"

"He's just trying to get us to look at the piece in a different way," Todd says. "He's trying to reach us on many levels. I'll tell you the truth, if I had to just listen to him read a poem and then tell me what it meant, I'd be bored to tears. I love that we get to actually interact with the piece."

Willard jokes and says, "Man, you interact on a date, not with a piece of poetry." They all laugh as they say their good-byes for the day.

The next class period is the strangest one yet to Melodie. When Professor North enters the room, he hands everyone a sheet of paper with a brief poem on it. He puts a CD in the boom box that he has brought, and he gives every student a huge lump of sculpting clay. "Today," he says, "I want you to read this brief poem, listen to the music I've brought while you read it, and then sculpt the poem with the clay I brought you. Any questions?"

Melodie is so stunned that she can't even think of a question. She begins to read the poem and listen to the music. She feels herself getting angry and stressed as tears come to her eyes.

Case Study Analysis

Name _____ Date _____

Class _____ Section _____

1. What are the **facts** you KNOW about the case?

   _____

   _____

   _____

2. What are some **logical assumptions** you can make about the case?

   _____

   _____

   _____

3. What are the **problems** involved in the case as you see it?

   _____

   _____

   _____

4. What is the **root problem** (the main issue)?

   _____

   _____

5. What do you estimate is the **cause of the root problem**?

   _____

   _____

6. What are the **reasons** that the root problem exists?

   _____

   _____

   _____

7. What is (are) the **solution(s)** to the problem?

   _____

   _____

   _____

8. Are there any **moral and/or ethical considerations** to your solution?

9. What are the **consequences** of your solution?

10. What are the **"real-world" implications** for this case?

11. How will the **lives** of the people in the case study **be changed** because of your proposed solution?

12. Where are some **areas on campus** that one could get help with the problems associated with this case?

13. Where are some **areas beyond the campus** that one could get help with the problems associated with this case?

14. What **personal advice** would you give to Melodie?

This Is a Test, This Is Only a Test

Calista loves school more than anything. She has always loved studying, working on projects, and writing. Her only problem is test taking. She is not comfortable with any type of tests, and over the years this has caused many academic problems. The problem is not that Calista doesn't study; the problem is anxiety and fear when the test begins. Despite her test-taking problems, she manages to do well in high school because she is an excellent writer and her work on projects and group activities is beyond reproach.

Calista faces several problems in her first semester of college, however. First, she registers for Dr. Maryanne Clyborne's History 101, The History of Western Civilization. The very first day of class, Calista finds that Dr. Clyborne gives only two tests: a midterm and a final exam. Period. There are no projects, no group work, and no extra credit. The tests are solely multiple choice and true/false. Calista thinks about dropping the course, but many of the other sections are already closed. She decides to remain in Dr. Clyborne's 101 class.

Calista is also taking English 101, Biology 110, Psychology 101, and Math 113. She is not worried about English because she writes so well. Biology poses a minor problem because there will be three lecture tests, but she is taking Biology Lab and this will help her grade. Psychology 101 scares her until she arrives for the first class and finds that there will only be one final, written exam and that the remaining grades will come from group projects and written essays. Calista has always done well in Math, so Math 113, Introduction to Algebra, looks like a breeze.

"So," she thinks, "if I can make it through History 101, three tests in Biology, and a written final in Psychology, I'll be fine." As the semester progresses, Calista does well in Math, Biology, and English. However, she scores a 71 on her first test in Psychology, and her midterm in History is only two weeks away. Her fear is already growing. She spends at least one hour each day studying her notes and rereading the chapters in her History text, and she even attends a study group for History once a week.

"I've got to do well," she thinks. "There are only two grades, and this one test is worth 50 percent of my final grade. "What if I black out?" she thinks. "What if I don't know the answer to the first question on the test, and the remaining questions are tied to the answer for question one?" Her inner voice continues. "What if I oversleep and miss the exam totally?" She is suddenly overcome with panic. "I know this is irrational," she thinks, "but so much is riding on this grade . . . this one grade."

Calista attends the last study session before the exam. The group brain-storms about possible questions, reviews the study sheet given to them by the professor, answer the questions at the end of each chapter, and plays a jeopardy game to quiz one another on the material. Calista does very well. She misses only one date and one location. Academically, she is ready for the test. Emotionally and mentally, she worries if the same old problems from high school will plague her.

The day of the test arrives, and Calista feels much more anxious than usual. She awakes early, has a good morning run, eats a bowl of hot cereal, and returns to her room to review her notes one more time. She leaves for class half an hour early just to calm her nerves. She enters the room at 10:15, and the class begins at 10:30. The professor hands out the exam and goes over the directions. "You have one hour and 15 minutes to complete the exam. Good luck."

Calista reads the first question.

1. The cradle of Western civilization was:

   a. Egypt.

   b. Mesopotamia.

   c. Greece.

   d. Turkey.

   e. Africa.

Immediately, Calista knows the answer. She puts down answer b and moves on to question two. "But wait," the voice in her head says. "Isn't Mesopotamia in Africa? Could this be a trick question? Does she mean the whole continent?" The voice is powerful. She goes back and erases her answer and tries to concentrate on question two.

2. _____ was the king of the Franks and Roman emperor.

   a. Leo III

   b. Julius Caesar

   c. Charles I

   d. Charlemagne

   e. Both b and d

Calista can barely breathe she is so nervous. "Roman emperor," she thinks. "Who was that?" The panic rises. She pauses for a moment. "OK, calm down and relax," she tells herself. "You know this stuff."

At 11:40, the professor calls for the exam. Calista looks up to realize that she is one of only three people left in the room. She hands in her exam although she knows that she has left three questions blank. She worries that she left some answers blank, and that she had to guess on some of them because the answers were so similar.

At the end of the next class period, the professor returns the exam. Calista waits until she is outside to unfold the paper. 58! "Oh, God," she thinks. "What am I going to do? How could this happen? I'm never going to get a college degree. How could this happen?"

Calista sits down on a bench near the Humanities Building to look over the exam. She can now see why she missed every question marked in red. "I knew that one!" she thinks. "Why did I go back and change my answer?" She looks at the answers that were similar and sees clearly what was really meant by the question. She feels stupid and angry for having done so poorly. "I guess I just need to drop the class," she thinks.

As she walks by the Records Office on the way back home, she pauses outside the door, trying to decide what to do.

Case Study Analysis

Name _____   Date _____

Class _____   Section _____

1. What are the **facts** you KNOW about the case?
   _____
   _____
   _____

2. What are some **logical assumptions** you can make about the case?
   _____
   _____
   _____

3. What are the **problems** involved in the case as you see it?
   _____
   _____
   _____

4. What is the **root problem** (the main issue)?
   _____

5. What do you estimate is the **cause of the root problem**?
   _____

6. What are the **reasons** that the root problem exists?
   _____
   _____
   _____

7. What is (are) the **solution(s)** to the problem?
   _____
   _____
   _____

109

8. Are there any **moral and/or ethical considerations** to your solution?

_____

_____

_____

9. What are the **consequences** of your solution?

_____

_____

_____

10. What are the "**real-world**" **implications** for this case?

_____

_____

_____

11. How will the **lives** of the people in the case study **be changed** because of your proposed solution?

_____

_____

_____

12. Where are some **areas on campus** that one could get help with the problems associated with this case?

_____

_____

_____

13. Where are some **areas beyond the campus** that one could get help with the problems associated with this case?

_____

_____

_____

14. What **personal advice** would you give to Calista?

_____

_____

_____

His Cheatin' Heart

Niles and Sonny file into the auditorium at Our Lady of the Pines College with the other 375 first-year students. The orientation is mandatory and is billed as an "interactive informational meeting." As the remaining students take their seats, the president of the college, Dr. Warren Fillmore, walks to the lectern and begins the opening session.

"Welcome to Our Lady," he begins. "Today is the first day of the rest of your life. Today may also be the last. I encourage each and every one of you to take your studies seriously and remember that this institution was founded on faith, fairness, rigor, and honesty. I expect no less of this class." He takes his seat behind the lectern, and suddenly a piano begins to play. An older gentleman approaches the microphone and asks that everyone stand and sing Our Lady's alma mater. "You'll find the words in the packet you were handed upon entrance."

"I didn't know it would be this formal," Niles says to Sonny. "We should have dressed better." They both laugh and begin to sing along to a song they had never heard before. When the song ends, everyone takes a seat and the president returns to the lectern. "Today, we have with us Dr. Randolph Chesterfield, our vice president of academic affairs. Dr. Chesterfield."

"Good morning," Dr. Chesterfield begins. "As President Fillmore stated earlier, this college has a long and rich history in this community, in this state, and in the higher education community. We are a faith-based, honor code institution, and we will expect full compliance with both orders. This morning, I plan to discuss our honor code and its ramifications for you."

Sonny leans over to Niles and says, "Jeez, you'd think we are Sing Sing." Again, they laugh until several students turn to them and shush them. They begin to realize that this is serious business. Everyone in the auditorium is extremely quiet and serious. Dr. Chesterfield says, "As an honor code college, you are expected to follow the guidelines set forth by the faculty, administration, and Board of Trustees. That code demands that you act in an honorable fashion in every aspect of your life and that you report anyone or any activity that is contrary to that policy." He continues, "The honor code that you will sign today states that you will not engage in any activity that reflects poorly on this institution, this community, on yourself, or your peers. It states that you will not plagiarize any document, that you will not cheat on any paper, test, or project, and

that you will obey all rules set forth by this institution. Failure to do so will result in your immediate and permanent termination from Our Lady of the Pines. *Also*, if you knowingly fail to report any act that is contrary to our honor code, you, too, will be permanently removed."

The tension can be felt in the air; not one word is uttered by the students or the faculty, although Niles can feel himself wanting to make a snide comment to Sonny. "In conclusion," Dr. Chesterfield lectures, "I expect every person of every age in this auditorium to conduct him- or herself with the utmost dignity in this educational process. Your honor code cards are on tables in the lobby, and you will need to read them fully and sign them today." The piano begins again as the older gentleman asks everyone to stand and sing the National Anthem.

Things progress well for the first few weeks of school. Niles and Sonny become closer and decide that they will request to be roommates for the next semester. They have only one class together this semester but plan to work their schedules for the next semester so that they are taking some of the basics at the same time.

One Thursday evening, Niles and Sonny are in the library studying for their Biology test the next day. Biology is the only class that they have together. They compare notes, create quiz cards, and query each other on terms that the professor said would be on the test. Niles is doing well with the questions, but Sonny does not seem to grasp the material. "I'm just no good at this," he says to Niles. "If I wanted to know this stuff, I'd have majored in Biology."

"Just relax," Niles tells him. "We've got a couple more hours to go. Just concentrate on what I'm telling you, and you'll be fine."

"I'm not gonna be fine," Sonny states nastily. "I've never been fine when it comes to Math and Science. I just don't get it."

"All you have to do is learn enough to get through the test, and then we can begin to prepare for the next test earlier."

"For me to pass a Biology test," Sonny says, "we'd have to have begun last year."

Friday morning rolls around, and they meet outside the Science Building. Niles has been up for two hours reviewing his notes. Sonny looks haggard and tired. "Did you sleep?" Niles asks.

"Some," Sonny says. "I tried to read over this crap again."

"We're going to make it, buddy. Just concentrate and take your time. We have 50 minutes to do the test. Don't rush. I'll meet you here after the exam."

They enter the classroom and take their seats. Other students are talking about the exam and questioning one another on some of the harder material. Sonny can feel the nervousness rising in his body. He feels stressed and afraid. The professor enters, asks if there are any last-minute questions, and hands out the test. "You have 50 minutes," he instructs. "I'll be back at the end of class. If you complete your exam before then, leave it right here on my desk face down. Good luck."

As the students begin, Dr. Cooke leaves the room and closes the door. There is complete silence besides the occasional grunt or moan. Shortly into the test, Niles looks over to Sonny's desk and sees a white 3×5 index card peeping from under his test paper. He can't believe what he sees and thinks that it must be the corner of another sheet of the test. Moments pass; he again looks at Sonny's desk and there it is, a white card with tiny notes scribbled all over both sides of it. He sees Sonny slip the card over and slide it back under his test. He can hardly believe what he is seeing. "Surely he would not resort to this," Niles thinks to himself. "How could he be cheating, knowing that he'll be kicked out of college?"

During the remainder of the test, Niles continues to look in Sonny's direction to see if he has made a mistake. Just when he has convinced himself that Sonny would have never done such a thing, Sonny takes the card and very quietly and quickly folds it in half and puts it in his shirt pocket. He gathers his belongings, leaves his test on the professor's desk, and leaves the room.

After Niles completes the test, he walks to the front of the Science Building, where he and Sonny had agreed to meet. "Wow, man," Sonny beams. "That was a killer test, but you were right. I took my time and I think I did OK." Niles does not say a word. "How did you do?" Sonny queries. Again, Niles is deathly quiet. "What's wrong, man?" Sonny asks. "Did you flunk it?"

"I saw what you did, Sonny," Niles says accusingly. "I saw your little card, so I'm pretty sure you did do well."

"I didn't have any card," Sonny says in the most serious voice.

"I SAW IT!" Niles almost screams. "I saw you using a cheat sheet, and here it is," he says loudly as he pulls the note card from Sonny's shirt pocket. "What is this, huh? Did Our Lady of the Pines just happen to put that little help sheet in there for you?" Niles asks sarcastically.

"I used that this morning on the way to class," Sonny whines.

"I don't want to talk to you right now, man," Niles says angrily. "You've put us both in horrible jeopardy. How could you do this to yourself? . . . *How* could you do this to me?"

Case Study Analysis

Name _____ Date _____

Class _____ Section _____

1. What are the **facts** you KNOW about the case?

   _____

   _____

   _____

2. What are some **logical assumptions** you can make about the case?

   _____

   _____

   _____

3. What are the **problems** involved in the case as you see it?

   _____

   _____

   _____

4. What is the **root problem** (the main issue)?

   _____

   _____

5. What do you estimate is the **cause of the root problem**?

   _____

   _____

6. What are the **reasons** that the root problem exists?

   _____

   _____

   _____

   _____

7. What is (are) the **solution(s)** to the problem?

   _____

   _____

   _____

8. Are there any **moral and/or ethical considerations** to your solution?

_____

_____

_____

9. What are the **consequences** of your solution?

_____

_____

_____

10. What are the **"real-world" implications** for this case?

_____

_____

_____

11. How will the **lives** of the people in the case study **be changed** because of your proposed solution?

_____

_____

_____

12. Where are some **areas on campus** that one could get help with the problems associated with this case?

_____

_____

_____

13. Where are some **areas beyond the campus** that one could get help with the problems associated with this case?

_____

_____

_____

14. What **personal advice** would you give to Niles?

_____

_____

_____

Adversity

at an early age. She and her husband, Jamal, have three young children, so going to school is very dif...

AT A GLANCE

George Washington Carver, the great African-American educator, once said, "I
have learned that success is to be measured not so much by the position that
one has reached in life, but by the obstacles which he has
overcome while trying to succeed."

Adversity can be one of the best and most cruel teach-
ers on earth. Adversity can be painful and horrific, but in the end, it is always
up to us how we use that adversity for the advancement of humanity.

At a Glance

CASE 1   Wave Good-bye to a 4.0

Harrison leaves the Midwest for a Pacific Coast university to study Marine Biology. He is engulfed in the beauty of California, the ocean, and his life. His roommate, Marcus, is a native Californian and loves to surf and enjoy the water. While Harrison is serious about his studies, Marcus is more interested in the next wave. He teaches Harrison to surf and enjoy the ocean from another perspective. Will Harrison catch the next wave or the next bus home?

CASE 2   Hurry Up and Wait, Please!

Julia is excited to be going to college, but if her first day is any indication of the years to come, she would just as soon go home now. From waiting in the wrong line at the bookstore to a mistake by financial aid that costs her hours of time, Julia's first day goes from bad to worse. Will she get past her anger and stay?

CASE 3   Give Me Strength

Tamika is an African-American woman who has finally gotten an opportunity to return to college. She has always been an excellent student and loved school, but she made the decision to get married at an early age. She and her husband, Jamal, have three young children, so going to school is very difficult for her. However, she is determined to complete her lifelong dream of getting a college degree.

Wave Good-bye to a 4.0

Harrison Dyer embraces his best friend, Todd Spellman, as the graduating class of Miller High School strolls out of the auditorium. All 57 graduates plan to attend a barbeque at the home of the principal later that evening. As Harrison and Todd greet other classmates with cheers and yells, Harrison feels a quiet sadness stir within him. He is glad that high school is over, but sad that he will be leaving Kansas in a few months to study Marine Biology at the University of California, Los Angeles. His sadness is magnified because neither Todd, Maria, Cynthia, nor Dwight, his closest friends for 12 years, is going with him. He knows that life is about to serve up a platter of major change.

In early August, Harrison packs his Toyota and leaves central Kansas for Los Angeles. First-year orientation is only two weeks away. Harrison plans to drive to Los Angeles, spend a couple of nights in a hotel, explore the city, and move into the residence hall on August 18. The plan is laid.

The drive goes off without a hitch. The scenery is breathtaking, and Harrison's first view of the Pacific is beyond words. His first day in Los Angeles, Harrison drives down Sunset Boulevard until the busy road ends at the ocean's lip. He parks the car, takes a deep breath, and walks along the coast for hours. As hard as it was to leave his friends and family, Harrison feels as if he is home.

After moving into the residence hall, attending orientation, registering for five classes, and going to a Campus Club rally in the Student Center, Harrison decides that he will not join any clubs his first semester. He wants to concentrate on his studies and get acclimated to the campus and his new life.

His roommate, Marcus, is a native Californian, a died-in-the-wool surfer, and a totally laid back guy. While their backgrounds are extraordinarily different, they hit it off quite well. "If you love the ocean, dude, you're a friend of mine," Marcus tells Harrison shortly after they meet. While Harrison is not a surfer, he and Marcus do have quite a bit in common. They both love sports, enjoy the company of friends, and could talk for hours about most things related to the ocean. Things are going well, better than Harrison ever imagined.

Two weeks into the semester, Harrison comes back to the room after an outing with his Biology class. Marcus is sitting on the bed with a huge smile on his face. "I got you something today," he says.

"You got me something? What is it?"

"Go open your closet door, man. You're gonna love it," Marcus says in a voice full of excitement.

Harrison walks over to the closet door, opens it, and gasps. "Oh my God, man! Where did you get this? I can't afford this," Harrison says.

"You don't owe me anything, man. It belonged to my older brother. I asked him if I could have it, and he said yes. It's an old one, man, but it still floats. Congratulations on your first surfboard."

"Wow," Harrison says. "I can't believe it. But I told you I don't even know how to surf. I've never done it before."

"I know that, roomie, but we're gonna fix that tomorrow. Tomorrow, you get your first surfing lesson. We'll go to the beach around 9:00 A.M., and I'll show you just what to do."

"I'd love to, Marcus, but I have History and English tomorrow morning. We can go about 2:00."

"Oh, no, my man, we're going in the morning. That is when the waves are best. You can just cut class tomorrow. . . . It's just one day. This is something you'll love forever.

"I can't . . . ." Marcus cuts him off.

"It's a done deal, man. We're going. You'll thank me later when you see how free surfing makes you. You can't be a marine biologist and not surf. That's as bad as a banker who doesn't golf. We go at 9:00, and that's final."

The next morning, Harrison and Marcus head off to the beach with their surfboards attached to the roof of Marcus's car. When they get there, Marcus shows Harrison how to sand his board, how to stand on it, how to use the ankle strap, and how to recover after a wipeout. Shortly after the first lesson, Harrison heads to the water and begins working the board in the water. "He's up!" Marcus yells. "Now he's down. Good job, man. Head back out and do it again."

This continues for the better part of the morning. Harrison is getting the hang of the board and realizes what Marcus was saying about the freedom of being on the board in the ocean. He is hooked.

When Harrison returns to History and English during the next class period, he finds that he missed a group editing project grade in English and a pop quiz in history. "How could this happen?" he thinks. "It was just one day." He finds a person from whom to get the history notes, but he can barely read the handwriting. He goes to the professor during office hours to see if he can make up the quiz, but Professor Peronne denies his request. "Pop quizzes are for class, not for makeup, young man." Harrison is upset that he missed two grades, but he rationalizes that he can catch up later.

Several weeks later, Marcus informs Harrison that he and five other buddies are going surfing again, and they ask him to come. He and Marcus have gone over the past two weekends, and Harrison is more hooked than ever. Actually, he is getting very good at surfing. "When are we going?" Harrison asks.

"In the morning, man. Pack your bags."

"Why would I pack my bags?" Harrison asks.

"'Cause we're heading up the coast to Santa Cruz. You're gonna love the waves up there, man. We'll be gone for four days. We're staying at Charlie's dad's house. It won't cost you a thing except for food."

"I can't do that, man. You know I have class, and you do too. How can we leave on a Tuesday and miss three days of classes?" Harrison asks impatiently.

"'Cause this is life, man; we only get one."

"I have to stay here. I've got a paper due, a group . . ." Marcus interrupts him.

"Dude, you're going and that's that. You can make all of that stuff up. You can't make up a wave."

"I . . ." Harrison is cut off again.

"Ach . . . umph . . . nah . . . No excuses."

Harrison is worried, but in his heart, he really wants to go. Later that evening, he packs his bag, and the next morning, the five guys head to Santa Cruz. Harrison has one of the best times of his life. He is amazed that a Kansas boy can surf, that he has made such great friends, that he is exploring the California coast, and that he feels connected. He worries about his classes, but he thinks, "Marcus is right. This is real life and real fun. You can't make this up."

Over the course of the next month, Harrison and Marcus surf more than they go to class. Harrison convinces himself that since he has missed enough projects and tests to knock him out of an A or B, he might as well enjoy the rest of the semester and have a good time doing what he loves.

At the end of the semester, Harrison has one C, two D's, and two F's. His grade point average is 1.25. When he opens his grade envelope, a bright yellow slip is included: "This is to inform you that because of your grade point average, you have been placed on academic probation."

Case Study Analysis

Name _____ Date _____

Class _____ Section _____

1. What are the **facts** you KNOW about the case?

_____

_____

2. What are some **logical assumptions** you can make about the case?

_____

_____

_____

3. What are the **problems** involved in the case as you see it?

_____

_____

_____

4. What is the **root problem** (the main issue)?

_____

_____

_____

5. What do you estimate is the **cause of the root problem**?

_____

_____

_____

6. What are the **reasons** that the root problem exists?

_____

_____

_____

_____

7. What is (are) the **solution(s)** to the problem?

_____

_____

_____

8. Are there any **moral and/or ethical considerations** to your solution?

9. What are the **consequences** of your solution?

10. What are the **"real-world" implications** for this case?

11. How will the **lives of the people in the case study be changed** because of your proposed solution?

12. Where are some **areas on campus** that one could get help with the problems associated with this case?

13. Where are some **areas beyond the campus** that one could get help with the problems associated with this case?

14. What **personal advice** would you give to Harrison?

Hurry Up and Wait, Please!

Julia finally completes the registration process for her five classes at Masters University in Oklahoma. This is her first semester, and things are not going as smoothly as she hoped they would have. She has trouble registering for her classes because she does not have an advisor's signature on her registration form. She waits in the wrong line for over an hour only to find out that she has completed the wrong form, and she has a verbal confrontation with a clerk in the Bursar's Office. "It is just not a good day," she says to herself as she heads to the bookstore to purchase her books and supplies.

She begins her search for her books and is amazed that something is finally going right today. "All of my books are here," she thinks to herself. "This is unbelievable after the day I've had." She gathers her seven books and heads to the checkout counter. She approaches the clerk, who asks whether she will be paying with check, cash, or credit card. Julie tells her that she will be paying with a scholarship voucher from Financial Aid.

"You're in the wrong line for that, honey," the clerk says. "You'll have to move over to register six."

"Why are there no signs to tell us that?" Julia asks unpleasantly.

"I just work here, honey. I don't make signs. I just run my register and know that I'm not set up to take scholarship vouchers. Next."

Julia moves to register six and is the eleventh person in line. There is only one clerk accepting scholarship vouchers. The line moves slowly, but she at least knows that she's in the correct line now. Twenty minutes pass, and finally Julia places her books on the counter. The clerk asks to see her voucher, and Julia hands it to her. The clerk types several codes into the computer and has a puzzled look on her face. She types in more numbers and moans a little. Finally, the clerk says to Julia, "Miss, I'm afraid that your voucher code is invalid. I'll have to call our manager."

Julia hears students behind her grunting and speaking impatiently. "Mr. Collins, register six, please." They all wait patiently. "Why is my code not working?" Julia asks the clerk.

"Sometimes the person in the scholarship office forgets to enter the data into the computer and the letter is no good without the code in the computer." At that moment, Mr. Collins arrives. "What's the problem?" he asks.

"I can't get her voucher code to come up," the clerk says. Mr. Collins enters a few numbers and hands the voucher back to Julia.

"I'm sorry, but our computer doesn't recognize this code as valid and we can't authorize a purchase without a valid code."

"What am I to do?" Julia asks.

"You'll have to go over to the scholarship office and have them re-enter the code from their office," he says.

"Why can't you do it here?" she asks. "You've got my code on the letter. Why don't you just enter it?"

"We don't have access to that screen," Mr. Collins says.

"But I've waited in two lines now for over an hour and still can't get my books."

"Well, you can pay cash for them and have the scholarship office reimburse you later," he says.

"But I don't have $400 for books," she says angrily. At that moment, she hears a student from the voucher line tell her to move on.

Julia steps out of line, places her books on the end of the clerk's counter, and walks out of the store. "I can't believe this," she says to herself. She can feel her anger, frustration, and stress rising. "This place just can't get it together," she thinks. She begins her journey over to the scholarship office, thinking, "This ain't gonna be pretty."

As Julia reaches the scholarship office, she is told to take a number from the number tab machine. Her number is 71. The next person called is 52. She can feel her face turning red. She approaches the receptionist's desk and tries to explain the situation to her.

"I was just here this morning, and someone forgot to put my code in the computer," she says nicely. "Can't you help me out here? I have my letter and everything, but the bookstore can't access the voucher."

"I can't do anything, Miss," the receptionist says, "You'll have to see an aid advisor."

"But I SAW ONE THIS MORNING," she says in a loud, stern voice.

"Miss, someone will be with you soon. I don't have access to the voucher screen out here. A counselor will help you as soon as one can."

Julia takes a seat with the other students waiting in the small lobby. Number 53 is called, 54, 55, 56, 68, 70, and finally, 71. Julia has been waiting for over an hour at this point. She rises and walks through the door to the back part of the scholarship office. She is met by Robin Greenly, who asks what she can do to help.

Julia explains the situation, shows her the letter from the morning's visit, and in less than thirty seconds, Robin has corrected the situation. "You're done," she says. "You can go back to the bookstore, and things should be fine."

"Why couldn't the bookstore or your receptionist help me?" Julia asks. "I've wasted over two hours on this and still have no books."

"They don't have access to the voucher screen," Robin tells her.

"Don't you think that it would be good to give them access to the voucher screen?" Julia asks curtly.

"Maybe," Robin says. "That's out of our hands."

As Julia feels her anger rising again, she takes the letter from Robin's hand, walks to the door, and leaves the building. She heads back to the bookstore. When she arrives, she is greeted by a security guard who directs her to a rather long line outside the front door. "You'll have to wait in line," the security guard says. "We've got a rush right now and the store is full to capacity."

"How long does it take to get inside?" Julia asks.

"Right now, we're running about an hour," he replies. "You can just wait over there."

"But I was here earlier and needed to get a voucher entered. I already have my books sitting on the clerk's counter," Julia explains.

"Sorry, Miss, you'll have to wait like everyone else."

Julia takes her place in line with the other students. She is angry, stressed to the max, hungry, tired, frustrated and, above all, saddened at the events of the day. Through her anger, she hears a voice ask, "How are you today?"

"You don't want to ask that right now," Julia replies to the student in front of her. "You *really* don't want to know."

Case Study Analysis

Name _____ Date _____

Class _____ Section _____

1. What are the **facts** you KNOW about the case?

   _____

   _____

   _____

2. What are some **logical assumptions** you can make about the case?

   _____

   _____

   _____

3. What are the **problems** involved in the case as you see it?

   _____

   _____

   _____

4. What is the **root problem** (the main issue)?

   _____

   _____

5. What do you estimate is the **cause of the root problem**?

   _____

   _____

6. What are the **reasons** that the root problem exists?

   _____

   _____

   _____

7. What is (are) the **solution(s)** to the problem?

   _____

   _____

   _____

8. Are there any **moral and/or ethical considerations** to your solution?

_____

_____

_____

9. What are the **consequences** of your solution?

_____

_____

_____

10. What are the **"real-world" implications** for this case?

_____

_____

_____

11. How will the **lives** of the people in the case study **be changed** because of your proposed solution?

_____

_____

_____

12. Where are some **areas on campus** that one could get help with the problems associated with this case?

_____

_____

_____

13. Where are some **areas beyond the campus** that one could get help with the problems associated with this case?

_____

_____

_____

14. What **personal advice** would you give to Julia?

_____

_____

_____

Give Me Strength

Tamika lives in a large northern city in a depressed neighborhood with her husband and three young children. Her husband has a factory job and works overtime as often as he can to earn more money for their family. Tamika works at nights as a waitress in a fast-food store close to home. One of her neighbors, Mrs. Tate, an elderly woman, cares for her children when she is at work. Although Tamika and Jamal work hard, their earnings are barely above minimum wage and they never seem to be able to get ahead. They've lived in a subsidized housing project all their married life. Tamika wants a better life for her children, and she is determined to set the example for them by going back to college. She wants to buy them a house in a nice neighborhood.

Quietly, without telling her family, she applies to a community college close by. She has decided to major in Math and Statistics because her teachers always told her that she was an excellent Math student. Besides, she has researched this major and she knows she can get a job making a very good salary. Getting a degree is very important to Tamika; making a good salary is imperative because she intends to send her own children to college. Tamika believes in the American dream, and she intends to experience it.

That night, she stays up late and waits for Jamal to come home from working overtime. She is tired from her job and taking care of the children. She always worries about her children when she is at work because Mrs. Tate is old and not able to do much with them. She wants to get them out of this neighborhood, where temptations are all around. She is already noticing that Marlene, who is 12, is using language that Tamika doesn't approve of and that her dress is becoming more provocative. She doesn't want her little boy Micah, who is the oldest son, to grow up around drugs and gangs and to be influenced by people who have no dreams and plans. She has to go back to school! And now she has to find a way to tell Jamal.

Jamal dropped out of school when he was only 14. His father died, and he had to go to work to support his mother and six siblings. Jamal is basically a good man. He loves his family, and he works hard for them. But he doesn't place much value on education, and he doesn't believe that his family can do much better than they are doing. Jamal still hangs out with his friends from this block. They tend to drink too much, and Tamika knows that he still occasionally uses drugs with his friends. She wants to get Jamal out of this neighborhood and try to change his values. She dreams of having him go back to school himself.

As she puts Jamal's food on the table, she makes small talk. She can tell he is not in a good mood, but she has to talk to him. School starts in two days and she has to get this over with, even though she knows his reaction may not be good. "Jamal, I have to talk to you about something," she begins. "You know how I was always good at Math in school and always loved school. Well, I want to go to college. I have been accepted into Jameson Community College, and I have a scholarship and financial aid. It won't cost us anything, and I can get a better job and we can do more for our family." The words pour out her mouth because she is nervous and afraid of his reaction.

As she expects, his reaction is not supportive. "Why don't you just forget about school? You always want to get away from who you are and where you came from. What's wrong with our neighborhood and our people? This is good enough for me, and it's good enough for my children. And I am tired of hearing about school all the time. You need to spend more time thinking about Marlene and what she's doing when you are not here."

Tamika is afraid, but she continues, "Well, I'm going to school, and I am going to make something of myself, and I am going to give my children opportunities I never had." She leaves the kitchen very upset and goes to bed, but she doesn't sleep well. She can smell the liquor on Jamal's breath when he finally comes to bed.

The next morning, Tamika talks to Marlene and her small children about school. She tells them she will not be at home on Tuesday and Thursday nights as she usually has been. In fact, between school and working as a waitress to help support the family, she will be gone every night. She tells Marlene that she will have to help Mrs. Tate more. To the smaller children, she says, "In the mornings, Mama is going to have to study, so you'll have to play together quietly." Of course, the children don't understand, but it makes her feel better to talk about it.

Marlene is sullen and resentful that she will have to take care of her siblings. "When do I get any time to hang with my friends? All I ever do is baby-sit and help Mrs. Tate. Why can't you just stay home and take care of us? You are the mother. I'm not!"

Tamika is hurt and upset, but she tries to explain to Marlene that she wants to go back to school to help her be able to have a better life—to go to college, to have nice clothes, to live in a better house. Marlene answers in a rebellious voice, "I like my friends right here in this neighborhood, and I'm not going to college. No one else goes to college around here. I'm going to drop out of school when I get to be 16, and you can't stop me. I'm getting a job in Daddy's factory and make money, so I can have a car and clothes like I want."

Heartsick with her family's attitude and tired from working all day with two small children and as a waitress the night before, Tamika, still determined, arrives on campus for her first class. She has enrolled in a Calculus class because she knows she can do well in this subject. Soon she forgets her troubles as she becomes absorbed in the teacher's lecture. "It feels so good to be back in school," she thinks. "I love to learn. I have to find a way to get my children to love learning and to get Jamal interested in getting his diploma. We can have a better life, but I have to get them turned around."

Excited and exhilarated at her evening, Tamika walks into a mess. Mrs. Tate was sick and didn't show up to keep the little children. Marlene put them to bed and went next door to be with her friends. At 10:00 P.M. she was still out. Jamal will be home soon, and the house is a wreck. Nothing has been prepared for him to eat, so he will be angry. She hears Micah crying and goes to his bed. He is sick and has a high fever. She holds him and talks to him. After giving him some medicine and getting him back to sleep, she goes into the kitchen to prepare Jamal's dinner. She is so tired and feels so guilty at having left her family to pursue her own dreams.

"Why can't my family understand how important this is for me? What made me think I could go to college and be somebody?"

Case Study Analysis

Name _____ Date _____

Class _____ Section _____

1. What are the **facts** you KNOW about the case?

_____

_____

2. What are some **logical assumptions** you can make about the case?

_____

_____

_____

3. What are the **problems** involved in the case as you see it?

_____

_____

_____

4. What is the **root problem** (the main issue)?

_____

_____

5. What do you estimate is the **cause of the root problem**?

_____

_____

6. What are the **reasons** that the root problem exists?

_____

_____

_____

7. What is (are) the **solution(s)** to the problem?

_____

_____

_____

8. Are there any **moral and/or ethical considerations** to your solution?

_____

_____

_____

9. What are the **consequences** of your solution?

_____

_____

_____

10. What are the **"real-world" implications** for this case?

_____

_____

_____

11. How will the **lives** of the people in the case study **be changed** because of your proposed solution?

_____

_____

_____

12. Where are some **areas on campus** that one could get help with the problems associated with this case?

_____

_____

_____

13. Where are some **areas beyond the campus** that one could get help with the problems associated with this case?

_____

_____

_____

14. What **personal advice** would you give to Tamika?

_____

_____

_____

Technology

In a rapidly changing world, technology is quickly becoming the common element that bonds us together. Recently, it was suggested that the new civil right is the ability to read. If we go deeper, however, the new civil right is really how well connected to technology we are. Computers have become a way of life for most Americans. Have we gone too far? Has technology damaged our ability to communicate with one another, or is technology opening new doors?

At a Glance

CASE 1 To Be Online or Not to Be Online . . . That Is the Question

Martha is elated to learn, quite by accident, that she can take all of her classes online, over the Internet. She decides to register for every class online so that she can work full-time and save some money. Things are going well until she misses a few assignments and runs into a high school friend who asks her about a social activity. Has Martha alienated herself from her college experience?

CASE 2 The Dark Side of the Web

Jake doesn't understand how Isaiah, a generally bright student, could become addicted to pornography on the web, but somehow he has become hooked. Nor can he understand how Alfonso, their other suitemate, can spend every waking minute on e-Bay trying to find the best deal on vintage baseball cards. Jake spends as much time in the suite as they do because he needs to keep track of the bets he has placed online. Aren't they in college? Aren't they supposed to be going to classes, meeting friends, and having the time of their life? Instead, they are locked up in their suite, chained to their computers. Will the Internet's dark side get the best of them?

CASE 3 Stop the World and Let Me Off

Malik attended a small, rural high school, where he performed very well. Despite the fact that his school was small, he had excellent teachers and he feels well prepared for college. He does leave for college somewhat concerned about his technology background because his high school was not as well equipped as some of the larger high schools in the state. Will he be left behind in a technologically advanced world?

To Be Online or Not to Be Online . . . That Is the Question

"If you've never considered taking an online class, it may be a solution to your time management, child care, work, and personal time problems," Dr. Rachel Bennington, the college's academic dean, tells the crowd of first-year students. "We offer an entire set of courses on the web, and we also offer five complete degrees. It may not be an option for everyone, but it may be just the thing that will help you get your degree. I hope you have a fantastic semester."

Martha leaves the auditorium and heads for her advisor appointment with Mr. Jones. She has never heard of an online course before. She decides that she will ask Mr. Jones about the classes and get his take on the pros and cons.

"An online class is very different from a 'traditional' class," Mr. Jones explains. "Most of them do not require any classroom time as you know it. You may have a chat session each week, but for most online classes, you do not go to a class with a professor and other students."

"Can I take any of my required classes online?" Martha asks.

"Yes, if they are open and your placement scores allow it, you can get your entire degree online if you want to," Mr. Jones answers.

"Wow," Martha says with surprise, "I've never even heard of this. I just sit at home, read what the professor requires online, attend the chat session, and turn in my papers? That's it?"

"Well, it sounds simple," Mr. Jones explains. "But many of the classes are harder online than they are in class. You have to be very dedicated and have a great deal of self-discipline. You can't just turn in everything at the end of the semester. Professors have time lines and due dates just like traditional classes."

"I think I want to try it, Mr. Jones," Martha says. "Can we see what is open?"

When Martha leaves Mr. Jones's office, she is registered for five online classes: English 101, Sociology 101, Study Skills 110, Math 125, and Religion 220. She is amazed that she will not have to come to campus at all this semester. "I can work during the days and take care of my classes at night," she thinks to herself. "This is unreal. I can even work overtime if I need to since I certainly need the money to help pay for tuition and my car insurance."

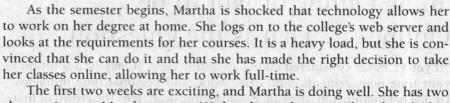

As the semester begins, Martha is shocked that technology allows her to work on her degree at home. She logs on to the college's web server and looks at the requirements for her courses. It is a heavy load, but she is convinced that she can do it and that she has made the right decision to take her classes online, allowing her to work full-time.

The first two weeks are exciting, and Martha is doing well. She has two chat sessions on Monday, one on Wednesday, and two on Thursday. She has learned how to maneuver through WebCT and has submitted two assignments on which she made A's. Shortly into the semester, she learns that the chat sessions are not required but are highly recommended. Her professors post the transcripts of the chat sessions the following day. If Martha misses a chat session, she simply logs on to the class site the next evening and reads word for word what was discussed during the chat.

During the fourth week of classes, Martha's boss asks her to work double shifts for the week to cover for an employee who is on vacation. Martha is happy to do so because she needs the money and her classes are going well. She does not attend any chat sessions that week. Her only worry is that she does not have time to check the chat logs to review the discussions. This puts her behind a little. Martha still feels confident that she can work as many hours as possible and maintain her grades.

After a week of double shifts, Martha logs on to her classes to discover that she has missed several important due dates for Sociology and Religion. She works very hard for two days to make up the work and submit the papers. She sends the papers to her professor by WebCT Private Mail. Later in the evening, she receives a notice from her Religion professor that he will not be able to grade the paper due to the missed deadline. The next morning, she receives a grade of 80 on her Sociology paper, but that grade is cut in half because it was not turned in on time. Her registered grade on the paper is 40.

Martha is devastated because she worked so hard on the papers. She logs on to her other classes to discover that because she spent so much time on the Sociology and Religion papers, she has nearly missed another deadline for English. She has a five- to seven-page paper due tonight. The "I" search paper is to be on a topic of her choosing. She spends a few hours online trying to find a topic and gather her research. By the time she writes the paper, she has no time to edit or rewrite the paper. She submits the paper as a first draft. When the paper is returned the next afternoon, the grade is 60/D. Martha is again devastated. She knows she is capable of so much more.

She catches up on a few more assignments, reads the chat transcripts, reads the assignments in her texts, and begins her newsletter project due the next week. The phone rings; it is Martha's boss. "Where are you?" he asks.

"I'm at home, Mr. Whitney. Why?"

"Because you're thirty minutes late for work, Martha," Mr. Whitney says.

"What do you mean?" Martha questions.

"Martha, you agreed to work for Cassandra this week. She left yesterday to be with her sister in the hospital. You have double shifts all week."

"Oh gosh, Mr. Whitney, I forgot. I'll be there in twenty minutes."

Martha is stunned that so much is happening at one time. She is behind in all of her classes, is committed to working another week of double shifts, and is beginning to doubt her ability to do all that needs to be done.

That evening while Martha is working, one of her friends from high school comes into the store. "Martha, where have you been?" Grace asks. "Are you in college this semester?"

"Yes," Martha explains, "I'm taking all of my classes online."

"That sounds wonderful," Grace says. "How is that going?"

"Fine," Martha says. "I have a lot of freedom to work and do things I need to do."

"Are you coming to the first-year student opener this weekend?" Grace asks.

"I didn't now about it," Martha says.

"Yes, we're all invited. It is going to be a blast. They have a live band and food and a salsa contest."

"I'll try to come," Martha says, knowing that she has to work.

"You should come and write for the newspaper," Grace says. "You did such a great job on the high school paper. Our advisor is wonderful. We're raising money to go to the Student Journalism Conference in Chicago next semester."

"That's wonderful," Martha says. "I'll try."

When Grace leaves the store, Martha feels sad that she is not connected to her class and college and that she isn't involved in any activities. She wonders if she has made the right decision.

Case Study Analysis

Name _____   Date _____

Class _____   Section _____

1. What are the **facts** you KNOW about the case?

   _____

   _____

   _____

2. What are some **logical assumptions** you can make about the case?

   _____

   _____

   _____

3. What are the **problems** involved in the case as you see it?

   _____

   _____

   _____

4. What is the **root problem** (the main issue)?

   _____

   _____

5. What do you estimate is the **cause of the root problem**?

   _____

   _____

   _____

6. What are the **reasons** that the root problem exists?

   _____

   _____

   _____

   _____

7. What is (are) the **solution(s)** to the problem?

   _____

   _____

   _____

8. Are there any **moral and/or ethical considerations** to your solution?

9. What are the **consequences** of your solution?

10. What are the **"real-world" implications** for this case?

11. How will the **lives** of the people in the case study **be changed** because of your proposed solution?

12. Where are some **areas on campus** that one could get help with the problems associated with this case?

13. Where are some **areas beyond the campus** that one could get help with the problems associated with this case?

14. What **personal advice** would you give to Martha?

The Dark Side of the Web

"You've got to be kidding me," Isaiah whispers to Jake during History 101. "You've never checked out all the hot babes you can find on the web? Dude, you are wasting your time on this earth!"

"MR. JEFFERSON," booms Dr. Fredrik Von Lichtenstein. "Would you like to share with the rest of the class what nuggets of brilliance you are imparting to your partner, seeing as how you believe they are far more important than what I am saying to the entire classroom?"

Jake sinks down in his chair wanting to die of embarrassment, but Isaiah boldly speaks up and says, "After your lecture on Monday about the Holocaust, you so inspired me to learn more about it that I got on the web and accessed a site called "The History Place.com" to learn more about this horrific event—dude, they even have pictures and stuff."

"Well, I'm quite impressed that you followed through and were encouraged to seek further information, even if it did come from the Internet. I am very familiar with The History Place website and it is credible, but I must warn the class about believing everything you read on the web," he cautions.

"The web is truly the last bastion for absolute freedom of speech. There is no censorship and relatively no consequences for printing illegal information or misinformation. It places a world of information at your fingertips, but with this suggestion comes a warning. There is no guarantee that the information is correct or factual. Anyone can put anything on the web and claim it as truth," Dr. Lichtenstein warns.

"On a personal note, I encourage you to watch the amount of personal information about yourself that you allow to be placed on the web. You will be amazed at what is already out there about you as an individual. Don't help them add to it by giving information to unprotected websites, and don't have a profile of yourself attached to your e-mails. Just a friendly warning." After that comment, class is dismissed for the day.

"Boy, did you think fast on your feet," Jake says to Isaiah.

"Well, I wasn't lying," says Isaiah. "I had actually gone to the site to check it out. The only lie was that we weren't talking about it at that moment. MissLily.com is more interesting," he grins.

Jake and Isaiah spot Alfonso, their other suitemate, on the way back to their room.

"Hey, what's up?" asks Alfonso.

"Isaiah was just about to tell us about Miss Lily.com. He found her while surfing the web last night," says Jake.

"Oh," says Alfonso, "well, she ain't got nothing over the mint condition Mickey Mantle baseball card I'm bidding on right now on e-Bay. Bids close in an hour, and I've gotta have it."

"Wait a minute, Alfonso, I thought you said you absolutely could not spend another dime on e-Bay this month," says Isaiah.

"I know," says Alfonso, "and I swore I wasn't going to, but then I signed on and my friend who's been following some of my dream items saw this one come up and I just *couldn't* pass it up."

"Yeah, like you couldn't pass up the Roger Maris mint condition card two weeks ago, or who was it the week before that?" asks Jake.

"Well, at least I'm not spending my parent's hard-earned money trying to hook up with an e-mail porn queen," says Alfonso. "How much are you into them for this week, Isaiah?"

"Not that much, and anyway mine's just for fun. I mean who wouldn't want to look at some bodacious babes? Man, they'll do just about anything you want them to do—it's incredible. They are so beautiful and hot and just waiting there for me every night when I turn on my computer. It's hard to turn it off at night," says Isaiah. "And anyway, I found out that they'll let me charge it to my phone bill once my credit card is maxed out."

"Uh, Isaiah, you do know these girls aren't real, don't you? They are just playing a role for money," says Jake.

"No, man, it's not like that. I've really made a connection with one of the girls. We send instant messages to each other. I mean, there is something special going on here. She needs me to be there every night for her, and I gotta be there for her . . . and for me," implores Isaiah.

Jake can sense his friend getting pretty tense about the conversation and tries to back off it a little bit. "OK, buddy, if that's what you say." Jake can't believe his friend is being hustled by an e-mail porn scam. Isaiah is generally a pretty bright guy, but he is losing it over this one and Jake is getting concerned. If that isn't enough to worry about, Alfonso is spending every cent he has on baseball cards while missing classes for fear he will miss a deal on e-Bay. He doesn't get it! Both of his friends are obsessed with the web, and he just doesn't understand it.

Everyone is using the Internet for classes and e-mailing, and, sure, most the guys on the hall spend some time cruising the porn sites every now and then, but not the way Isaiah does. Jake considers this as he enters his residence hall.

"Hey, Jake, how about a game of basketball this afternoon?" asks his RA Jason. "No, thanks," replies Jake. "I've got to study." He takes the stairs two at a time up three flights until he reaches his fourth-floor suite.

When he reaches his suite, Jake is amused but not surprised to see Alfonso and Isaiah already manning their stations. Isaiah is sitting on the couch with his laptop, while Alfonso is at the desk.

"Alright," says Jake. "I sure hope these teams cover the spread better than the dogs I chose last week."

"Hey, man, I thought you weren't going to be placing any bets this week?" asks Isaiah.

"Well, I've got to because I lost so much last week that I had to take out a loan from this guy who is a friend of a friend, if you get my drift, and I don't think he will take too kindly to my not paying him back—so I've got to win tonight," says Jake.

As Jake makes this comment, he looks up and stops. He does not realize that he has left the door to their suite slightly ajar and that their RA has followed him up. Isaiah and Alfonso continue on in their own little world, but Jake is stunned by the words he has just uttered and the scene the RA is witnessing. Two of his closest friends in the world are sitting in front of computers in a room that looks like a war zone. He's placing bets online, and it is obvious that they have been eating all of their meals, as well as sleeping, at the computers.

Jason, the RA, says, "Guys, I think we need to have a little talk." At this statement, Isaiah and Alfonso both jerk around, completely surprised to see him. They are oblivious to what has transpired for the past several minutes.

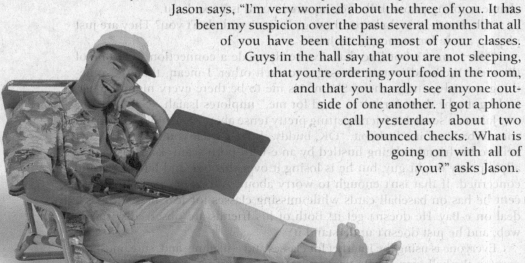

Jason says, "I'm very worried about the three of you. It has been my suspicion over the past several months that all of you have been ditching most of your classes. Guys in the hall say that you are not sleeping, that you're ordering your food in the room, and that you hardly see anyone outside of one another. I got a phone call yesterday about two bounced checks. What is going on with all of you?" asks Jason.

Case Study Analysis

Name _____   Date _____

Class _____   Section _____

1. What are the **facts** you KNOW about the case?

   _____

   _____

   _____

2. What are some **logical assumptions** you can make about the case?

   _____

   _____

   _____

3. What are the **problems** involved in the case as you see it?

   _____

   _____

   _____

4. What is the **root problem** (the main issue)?

   _____

   _____

5. What do you estimate is the **cause of the root problem**?

   _____

   _____

6. What are the **reasons** that the root problem exists?

   _____

   _____

   _____

7. What is (are) the **solution(s)** to the problem?

   _____

   _____

   _____

8. Are there any **moral and/or ethical considerations** to your solution?

_____

_____

_____

9. What are the **consequences** of your solution?

_____

_____

_____

10. What are the **"real-world" implications** for this case?

_____

_____

_____

11. How will the **lives** of the people in the case study **be changed** because of your proposed solution?

_____

_____

_____

12. Where are some **areas on campus** that one could get help with the problems associated with this case?

_____

_____

_____

13. Where are some **areas beyond the campus** that one could get help with the problems associated with this case?

_____

_____

_____

14. What **personal advice** would you give to Isaiah, Alfonso, and Jake?

_____

_____

_____

Stop the World and Let Me Off

Malik knows that he will have adjustment problems at college since he is leaving a small, rural high school with a nurturing environment. He knows all the teachers and their families, and they know his family. The principal calls all the students by name; the classes have been small; and the entire town is involved in supporting the athletics program. As he drives through the gates of the large university, he is more than a little nervous about the adjustment period that he knows is ahead of him. He is most concerned about his technology background because his school was underequipped with computer technology and the faculty was not as prepared as they might have been. He knows he will have to work very hard to catch up. Nevertheless, this is what he wants, and he is determined to adjust and to pay the price to keep up.

Malik goes through orientation and is pleased to meet other students with similar backgrounds. He spends his first afternoon in the bookstore in long lines, buying books for his first semester. Since many of the basic courses were already closed by the time Malik registered, he has enrolled in a course normally taken by sophomores. "You should be fine in this," his advisor told him as he rushed him out of his office.

Malik has chosen Journalism as his major and learns on his first day of class that he needs to pass a keyboarding proficiency exam. His heart jumps to his throat because he is not the best typist in the world. Fortunately, he passes, though barely, and he makes a mental note to get help in this area. Obviously, knowing how to type well and to use computers is going to be very important in his major.

He has no problems with his Math, English, History, and Psychology courses. "I can do well in all of these," he thinks to himself. Then he is off to his first Journalism course.

The professor begins with this announcement: "You are expected to know the basics of computer technology in this course. I will not teach you how to do word processing, database management, spreadsheets, Internet research, and so forth. You will be using the computer on a daily basis, and all homework and research will require the use of a computer. If you do not have a computer, I suggest you buy one since it is sometimes difficult to get a place in the laboratories. If you performed poorly on your keyboarding test, I suggest you go to the local community college and take a typing course. You will stay behind until you can use a computer efficiently." Malik thinks, "This is not friendly old Mrs. Wharton."

The professor continues, "The most important characteristic of this society we live in may well be the incredible speed with which it changes. This change might be good or bad, but change is going to happen, and you have got to change with it or become obsolete yourself. What you learn in this class this semester relative to technology will be obsolete by the end of next semester unless you continue to build on your basic knowledge. I can tell you that even the best and most advanced groups of researchers, professors, and technologists often feel overwhelmed by the amazing changes in technology."

Malik feels afraid because he knows this professor is addressing him. "Oh, great! Just what I needed to hear when I am already scared to death. Can I keep up," he wonders, "or do I need to drop this course? But if I drop it, what will I pick up? My advisor already told me that most of the courses are closed, and he acted like he never wanted to see me again, much less this semester."

Malik misses his old school and its comforting environment. Back home, he could have gone to the counselor, and she would have taken care of his problems. Who can he turn to here? His advisor obviously doesn't want to be bothered.

His thoughts are interrupted by his professor, who is moving ahead at a phenomenal pace. "So let's get started. I want you to assume that you are working on an article about serial killers. You are to go to the Internet, find cases about serial killers, and see if there is anything that relates them and their practices to the case I am giving you now."

Malik thinks, "I think I can do that." Then the professor continues, "In addition, I want you to download pictures of the serial killers, any crime scene photos or forensic evidence you can find, and insert them in the draft of the document you are working on. Further, I want you to create a database of all your references, police who worked these cases, FBI agents and their contact information, and any other resources that you might use in writing about this case in such a way as to pique the public's interest. Oh, and one more thing, insert a table that illustrates the increase of crimes committed by serial killers in this decade and, particularly, this region of the country. You might make a comparison of the country as compared to this region.

"Now, let's move on. You will be required at the next class meeting on Thursday to make a five-minute presentation on what you have discovered. Your presentation should include the use of PowerPoint with appropriate animation and music to keep the attention of your colleagues. And you should, of course, download your Internet findings and insert them in your presentation for realism. You will also need to turn in your first draft of your article on serial killers. I will edit these over the weekend and return them to you in time to meet your deadline."

Malik knows he has died and woken up in hell. He doesn't have a clue how to do any of the last things the professor assigned. His thoughts are interrupted again by this professor who is intent on pushing him over the edge.

"And finally, let's get this straight from the beginning. All information taken from the Internet or any other sources must be documented. If you abuse this policy in any way and fail to document your resources, you will be given an automatic F in this course. I intend to make you journalists of the first order, and we will do things right in this course. Don't even think about falsifying information, no matter how glamorous it makes your article. Our job is to sell papers and information, of course, but it is first to tell the public the truth. We must give them honest information so they can make decisions that affect their lives and their philosophies. Any abuse of this policy will not be tolerated! Do I make myself clear?

"Now, you may begin your work on this project in class. I'll see you on Thursday. I'll be out of town for a conference until then. If you have questions, you can call Jackson, my graduate assistant. His number is on the syllabus." With that announcement, the professor turns on his heels and quickly exits the room.

Malik is so shaken that he hardly knows where to begin. "What can I do?" he thinks. "I don't have a clue how to do this. I have to have some help, and even then, I'm not sure I can learn this in time."

Case Study Analysis

Name _____ Date _____

Class _____ Section _____

1. What are the **facts** you KNOW about the case?

    _____

    _____

    _____

2. What are some **logical assumptions** you can make about the case?

    _____

    _____

    _____

3. What are the **problems** involved in the case as you see it?

    _____

    _____

    _____

4. What is the **root problem** (the main issue)?

    _____

    _____

5. What do you estimate is the **cause of the root problem**?

    _____

    _____

    _____

6. What are the **reasons** that the root problem exists?

    _____

    _____

    _____

7. What is (are) the **solution(s)** to the problem?

    _____

    _____

    _____

8. Are there any **moral and/or ethical considerations** to your solution?

_____

_____

_____

9. What are the **consequences** of your solution?

_____

_____

_____

10. What are the **"real-world" implications** for this case?

_____

_____

_____

11. How will the **lives** of the people in the case study **be changed** because of your proposed solution?

_____

_____

_____

12. Where are some **areas on campus** that one could get help with the problems associated with this case?

_____

_____

_____

13. Where are some **areas beyond the campus** that one could get help with the problems associated with this case?

_____

_____

_____

14. What **personal advice** would you give to Malik?

_____

_____

_____

Campus Safety

One of the most compelling issues on college campuses over the past decade
has been safety. Colleges work very hard to create safe environments
on campus, from escorts to emergency phones located throughout campus to video cameras in parking lots to better lighting.
Safety, however, is a two-way street. Individuals must also
play a significant role in their personal safety.

CASE 1   Who's Afraid of the Dark?

Heesun is an international student from Korea. She has a difficult time talking her parents into letting her go to school in the United States because they are worried about her honoring their traditions. They are also concerned about her safety on a large American university campus. She has promised faithfully to be careful and to use her best judgment regarding her safety. Her world is about to change.

CASE 2   The Time of Her Life

Alexia's best friend and roommate, Sandy, meets a guy, Daniel, on the web who convinces her to let him join them in Cancun for their spring break. Unbeknownst to Alexia, Daniel and Sandy have decided that it would be exciting to experiment sexually with a threesome, and Alexia is going to provide the third person with the help of a little tequila and some ecstasy.

CASE 3   Clubbed to Death

Hoppers is a jamming nightclub close to campus. Frequently, DJs from L.A., New York, Boston, and London are playing. A close group of students usually spends Friday nights there dancing and relieving the stresses from the week. This particular night, the girls meet a few guys who love to dance, flirt, and do a few drugs. Will this be the night that beauty meets the beast?

Who's Afraid of the Dark?

Heesun is so excited to be in this strange, new, wonderful land and equally happy to have the opportunity to attend a large American university. This has always been her dream, and she could not be more thrilled—until she begins trying to register and discovers that the first-year classes are almost booked up. Her choices are very limited, and she feels discouraged. Her advisor suggests that she consider evening school, which would greatly improve her selections.

Heesun remembers promising her parents that she will be especially careful in the evenings and wavers for a few seconds. Then she tells her advisor to sign her up for two evening courses because she is interested in getting the courses she needs for her major. She will be going to class four nights each week, beginning at 4:30 and finishing at 6:15.

In the beginning, Heesun doesn't mind the evening classes too much; in fact, she likes them because it gives her time to get her homework done and to exercise and meditate while her roommates are out of the suite. The safety problem doesn't seem to be that much of an issue at the beginning of the semester. Then the time changes back from daylight savings time. On the first evening after class following the time change, Heesun walks outside and is concerned to see that it is dark.

She looks all around. The parking lot is dark, and she has to walk all the way back to her dormitory, a 10-minute walk.

Heesun has always been afraid of the dark. By the time she reaches her dormitory, she is terrified. What is she going to do? She doesn't have a car, and she doesn't have any close friends who do. She is worried that she is breaking her promise to her parents, and she is frightened for her safety.

The next evening, she can hardly focus on her class because she is dreading going outside and having to make that walk alone. She looks around to see if she recognizes anyone that she can walk with back to the dorm. Most of the students are nontraditional students who are taking night classes. "Why," she asks herself, "did I decide to take evening courses?" The professor calls on her in the middle of her thoughts. She doesn't even hear the question and is embarrassed when he calls her name again. She has no idea what he has been discussing. Heesun, who has been taught to be very respectful of her professors, is humiliated. She stays afterward to apologize to the professor.

When she walks outside, she is more frightened than ever. Now, all the other students have vacated the building and the parking lot while she was talking to her professor. As she walks up the hill, she hears steps behind her. She is so scared that she starts running as fast as she can. Looking behind her, she sees that the person behind her is still walking at a normal pace. She feels like such a fool! But she doesn't slow down.

Back in the dorm, she tries to remember some of the tips that were given to the students during orientation. Why didn't she pay more attention when they were giving advice on night walking routes, an escort service, and other assistance? If only she knew who to call for help. It is hard to be alone and lost in a foreign country. Why didn't she pay more attention to that lecture on safety at orientation? "What did they say about phones along the pathways?" she asks herself.

Heesun tells her roommates about her fears, and they find her amusing. "Oh, Heesun, you are just exaggerating this issue. Chances are very slim that anything will happen to you. You are just afraid of the dark," they tease.

Determined to overcome her fears, Heesun continues her evening classes. She also continues to be afraid and ends up looking behind her all the way back to her dormitory. Several times she has been so sure someone was hiding in the shrubbery along the way. Her fears are beginning to affect her grades. She is, however, determined to get over her fears. She will not be defeated by her fears!

That night, when she gets back to the dorm, her roommates are out. One of them comes in about 10:00 P.M. from the library, but the other one is still out when they finally decide to go to bed. "Maybe we should call her on her cell phone," Heesun suggests. They are unable to reach her. "She's probably in a club somewhere. You know how she loves to dance," says Heesun's roommate. Reluctantly, they go to sleep.

When the girls awake the next morning, their roommate is not in her bed. They are panicky now. This is not like Marie. Yes, she will party with the best, but she is not irresponsible. At the risk of appearing overanxious, they decide to call campus police. Within minutes, the police arrive and begin questioning the girls. "Try not to worry," they say. "This happens all the time. She's probably out with her boyfriend." They know this is not true. Her boyfriend lives in another state. "We'll let you know if we locate her. You call us when she returns home, as she surely will." The campus police leave to search for their friend.

Around noon, when the roommates have returned to their dorm to eat lunch, they hear a knock on the door. The police officers are back, and they have another person with them. The roommates can tell that something is terribly wrong. The police tell them that their roommate has been found and that they have very bad news. "Marie has been found behind the student center, where she went to dance last night. We hate to tell you this bad news, but Marie has been strangled. She's dead." They almost collapse with the terrible news. She was just here yesterday, laughing and teasing Heesun about her fear of the dark. And now she has died on campus in a student-oriented location. The counselor accompanying the police offers to listen to them and to try to help them get through this terrible situation.

Heesun feels as though she can't breathe. Her worst fears have come true. What if her parents find out? They would never let her stay in this country. How can she go back to evening school now? She is more afraid than ever!

Case Study Analysis

Name _____ Date _____

Class _____ Section _____

1. What are the **facts** you KNOW about the case?

   _____

   _____

   _____

2. What are some **logical assumptions** you can make about the case?

   _____

   _____

   _____

3. What are the **problems** involved in the case as you see it?

   _____

   _____

   _____

4. What is the **root problem** (the main issue)?

   _____

5. What do you estimate is the **cause of the root problem**?

   _____

6. What are the **reasons** that the root problem exists?

   _____

   _____

   _____

7. What is (are) the **solution(s)** to the problem?

   _____

   _____

   _____

8. Are there any **moral and/or ethical considerations** to your solution?

_____

_____

_____

9. What are the **consequences** of your solution?

_____

_____

_____

10. What are the **"real-world" implications** for this case?

_____

_____

_____

11. How will the **lives** of the people in the case study **be changed** because of your proposed solution?

_____

_____

_____

12. Where are some **areas on campus** that one could get help with the problems associated with this case?

_____

_____

_____

13. Where are some **areas beyond the campus** that one could get help with the problems associated with this case?

_____

_____

_____

14. What **personal advice** would you give to Heesun?

_____

_____

_____

The Time of Her Life

Nausea creeps over Alexia as consciousness begins to clear the fog that had plagued her all night. As she awakes, she realizes that the pressure she feels on top of her is not a dream but a person. "I'm right here with you, baby," whispers a husky voice next to her ear.

Alexia screams and starts struggling against the weight on top of her. She is no longer dreaming but realizes she is pinned to the bed and a person is on top of her.

"Oh my God," is all she can think. "No, dear God, not this."

Somehow, she manages to dislodge her assailant. She rolls from the bed, grabs a glass, and throws it at him. She runs for the bathroom, where she locks herself in.

"What the hell," yells Daniel as he dodges the glass.

In the same bed on the other side of Daniel, Alexia's roommate and best friend, Sandy, sits up and asks groggily, "What's going on, Daniel?"

"I don't know. Your whacked-out roommate just woke up and started freaking out and throwing glasses at me. You told me she's cool with all this," says Daniel.

"I thought she was cool with it. Last night she was pretty wasted. I've never known the girl to be so completely loaded in all my life, but she seemed down with it," replies Sandy.

"Lexi," Sandy calls through the bathroom door. "Are you OK?" Only silence. "Lexi, you are worrying me. Open the door and let me talk to you. What's wrong?"

Finally, the door cracks and Alexia's face appears. Her blurry eyes and the tears do not jive with the normally bubbly and fun-loving Alexia that Sandy knows. "Who is he?" asks a clearly distraught Alexia.

"Who?" asks Sandy. "You mean Daniel? He's the guy I've been e-mailing forever. Remember, we decided to hook up while we were here in Cancun for our spring break. Come on, don't you remember we talked about it and then we all met last night in the bar? Of course, you had been doing shots of tequila for half the night before he showed up, so you were pretty wasted."

"What happened here last night?" asks Alexia.

"What do you mean what happened? You were here, stupid. We partied all night and had sex," replies Sandy.

Alexia can't believe it! She falls against the door sobbing and orders Sandy to make Daniel leave immediately and to have the housekeepers clean the room completely. Thoughts race through her head. "Sex with a total stranger; sex with a total stranger and her best friend; sex with a woman who was supposed to be one of her closest friends; what had she been thinking?"

Her memories of last night are sketchy at best, but she has no memory of sex. She thinks for a moment that Sandy is playing a joke on her. "If it is a joke," she thinks, "then how can I explain the very real sexual encounter this morning? My god, I'm not even sexually active, and Sandy knows this," thinks Alexia.

"Did we have safe sex?" Alexia whispers through the bathroom door.

"I can't remember," says Sandy. "I know at the beginning of the night I insisted, but Daniel kept complaining. I insisted back, but by then things were so crazy and we were all so drunk. I just don't know."

"Has this man been tested for sexually transmitted diseases?" Alexia asks.

"He said he had been tested and that everything is fine," Sandy replies.

"Have you been tested, Sandy?"

"Yes," came the reply.

"Well, I haven't," replies Alexia. "Oh my God. I'm so confused. Does this mean we are gay since we've had sex together?" The thoughts are becoming overwhelming, and Alexia begins to quietly cry.

"No, sweetie, we are not gay," says Sandy.

Being a participant in a three-way was never a part of Alexia's sexual plans. How had this happened? All she can remember about the night before is getting ready for an evening of partying. She and Sandy were supposed to meet some of their other friends from college who were staying in the same hotel over break. They were going to go clubbing. She can vaguely remember dancing with Alfonso and Tomas and sitting and doing some shots of tequila with Kiyoko and Caitlyn at this really trendy looking bar. She knows that Daniel met them there, but beyond that, her mind is blank.

Lexi feels incredibly dirty and sore, so she decides to take a shower. Climbing into the shower, she glances down at her body and is horrified to see several bruises around her breast and pubic areas, as well as what appears to be a bite mark on her right breast. Her ankles are both bruised as if they have been tied. The nausea she felt upon waking overcomes her and she ends up vomiting in the shower. Whatever happened the night before, it had not been gentle, nor had it been within her normal realm of sexual behavior.

As Alexia puts on her clothes, she hears voices in the bedroom and goes out to find Kiyoko, Caitlyn, and Destiny as well as Sandy sitting there chatting about the day's events, as if her world has not just been torn apart. "Hey, Lexi," says Destiny. "Hey, girl," chimes in Caitlyn and Kiyoko.

Sandy says, "I'll take my shower now," and hurries into the bathroom.

Destiny, never one to mince words, says, "Alright, girl, what in the world is going on in this room? The atmosphere is so tense, you could cut it with a knife."

It takes no more than that question for Alexia's thin control to break, and she begins crying hysterically while trying to tell her friends what happened the night before. The story is sketchy because her memory is hazy, but she is able to explain the gist of it.

"My god, Alexia, you were raped!" screams Kiyoko. "We've got to call the police."

"Wait a minute, Kiyoko, don't go freaking out on us and jumping to conclusions," says Destiny. "Lexi, calm down and tell me. Do you remember meeting Daniel?"

"Sort of, but then everything is a blank," screams Alexia. "All I remember is waking up with him on top of me—it was awful. I feel so dirty, so violated. How could Sandy do this to me? I trusted her. We've grown up together."

"OK," says Destiny, "we've just got to talk about this and see what we need to do." Just then, the bathroom door opens. Sandy begins, "You know, about this afternoon . . ."

Sandy's statement stops midstream as she surveys the scene in front of her.

"We know what happened here last night. We know how you set Alexia up to be an unwitting participant in a threesome with you and your sicko Internet boyfriend Daniel," says Destiny.

"Did you do any checking into his background before you decided to hit it with him? Do you even know if his real name is Daniel?" asks Caitlyn.

"I don't know about you guys, but it sounds to me like Lexi was drugged and then raped against her will," says Destiny.

"There is no way this was rape," Sandy says sternly. "Alexia knew what she was doing and she never said no, so how can that be rape? Lexi, hon, come on. I'd never do anything to hurt you. We can clear this up, please. I know this is embarrassing, but tell these guys that we got a little too wasted and things got outta hand."

Slowly, Alexia rolls over, stands up, and unties her robe. Beneath it, she is wearing nothing. She pulls it open to reveal the bruising, bite marks, and welts that are now becoming more prominent around both her wrists and ankles. It is now obvious to everyone that all is not well.

Case Study Analysis

Name _____ Date _____

Class _____ Section _____

1. What are the **facts** you KNOW about the case?

_____

_____

2. What are some **logical assumptions** you can make about the case?

_____

_____

3. What are the **problems** involved in the case as you see it?

_____

_____

_____

4. What is the **root problem** (the main issue)?

_____

_____

5. What do you estimate is the **cause of the root problem**?

_____

_____

_____

6. What are the **reasons** that the root problem exists?

_____

_____

_____

7. What is (are) the **solution(s)** to the problem?

_____

_____

_____

8. Are there any **moral and/or ethical considerations** to your solution?

_____

_____

9. What are the **consequences** of your solution?

_____

_____

10. What are the **"real-world" implications** for this case?

_____

_____

_____

11. How will the **lives** of the people in the case study **be changed** because of your proposed solution?

_____

_____

_____

12. Where are some **areas on campus** that one could get help with the problems associated with this case?

_____

_____

_____

13. Where are some **areas beyond the campus** that one could get help with the problems associated with this case?

_____

_____

_____

14. What **personal advice** would you give to Alexia?

_____

_____

Clubbed to Death

T

The music is jamming, the dance floor is hot, the crowd is mixed, and the energy in the room is electric. Everyone has been waiting for this night for weeks. It is the monthly DJ bash at Hoppers, a local club near campus. Posters advertise that it is the hottest ticket in town. DJs from L.A., Boston, New York, and London are scheduled to appear, with the hottest beats and the latest hits.

"Ya'll ready fah dis?" the DJ shouts as he takes the music to a higher level. The crowd goes wild. The club is so packed that you can't help but touch people as you walk from one area to another. It is a wild and free scene. There are no real couples on the floor; everyone is dancing with everyone. The beat doesn't stop, and the dancing doesn't either. Aya and Charla make their way to a corner of the room for a breather.

"Girl, it has got to be 110 degrees in here!" Charla yells.

"I'll hold our spot if you go get us a drink," Aya says.

"Hang tight, I'll be back."

Charla and Aya are great friends and enjoy coming to Hoppers weekly. To them, it is a great way to chill out after a stressful week of classes and working. They never go to the club without each other, and they usually meet four or five other friends there on Friday nights. Some of their friends come to the club two or three times a week. Tonight, however, is a special night. It is Tamara's birthday and the club is having a special DJ party. They decide that this is the perfect place to celebrate.

Charla returns with two sodas. One is only half full. "Girl, some guy over there is wearing half your drink." They laugh and relax for a moment before heading back to the crowded dance floor. After dancing for a while longer, they spot Tamara and two other friends on the floor. They make their way over to them, and the reunion is loud and joyous.

"Happy birthday, girl!" Charla yells. "Happy B-day, happy B-day, happy B-day."

They all hug and get into a big dance huddle. All of a sudden, the music stops. The DJ says, "This next beat goes out to Tamara on her 20th! You party down, lady!!" The music roars to full volume and so does the crowd.

"Oh, my God," she yells, "how did he know that?"

Aya says, "Some little birdie musta told him." They laugh and dance for another half hour or so.

Shortly before midnight, the girls are sitting at a table watching the crowd, catching their breath, and enjoying a drink. The five of them always have a great time at Hoppers. The crowd can get overly rowdy, and some violence has occurred in the back parking lot, but as a whole, the club is fairly safe. They suspect nothing different tonight.

As they sit and yell back and forth over the music, three guys approach the table. They ask if they can have a seat. The girls agree to let them join in once they discover that they go to the same school. Tamara and Aya agree to dance with two of the guys, while Charla and the remaining guy go to the bar to refresh everyone's drink. Monique and Jennifer stay at the table to save their place.

As Charla and Antonio wait in line at the bar, he extends his hand and says, "Want some?"

"Some what, man?" she asks.

"X, baby," he smiles. "X marks the spot."

"I don't do that stuff, man," she yells to him. "Bad for ya."

"Have you ever tried it?" he questions.

"Nah. I just know."

"You don't know nothing until you try," he says. "Take just half. You probably won't even feel half."

"But I've had two drinks already," she says.

"That's OK, baby. It just intensifies the drink and makes you feel like dancing," he says.

"I'm already dancin'," she yells.

"Come on, you do half and I'll do half."

She looks at him, smiles, and takes the X from his hand. Once they get their drinks, she puts the half pill in her mouth and takes a drink.

When they get back to the table, everyone is there. Each person takes a drink, and after a moment, everyone heads back to the dance floor. Monique agrees to stay and watch the table.

Shortly thereafter, Monique is approached by a guy who asks her to dance. She informs him that she is watching the table and can't dance until the group returns. He asks if he can stay and talk to her. She agrees. They talk for what seems to be an hour or so. They get along well, and she enjoys talking to him. She knows that he is just flirting with her, but she enjoys the attention.

"When are they coming back to the table so you can enjoy the floor, baby?" Keith asks.

"I don't know. Watch the table a sec, and let me get one of my girls to come back and we'll dance if you want to."

"That'll be great," Keith says.

Monique makes her way through the dance floor and finally arrives at the place where Aya, Charla, and the guys are dancing.

"Aya, will you come sit at the table for a while so I can dance with this cute, cute guy?" Monique asks.

"Soon as this track is over, we'll come over," Aya says.

Monique makes her way back to the table and tells Keith that her friend is coming back any moment.

When the song ends, Aya and Gregg come back to the table. Keith stands and pulls the chair out for Monique and says, "Drink up, girl, you're gonna be thirsty when this dance is over."

Monique smiles and winks at Aya, downs her drink, takes Keith by the hand, and is off to the floor.

Shortly afterward, Charla and Antonio come back to the table. Aya and Tamara can tell that Charla is high. "Whew, girl . . . it's HOT up in here," Charla yells. "Hot!"

"What you high on, Charla?" Tamara asks.

"Life, baby, we're high on life."

Antonio laughs as Charla runs her hands through his hair and down his chest.

"You better get high on some common sense, girl, before you get into trouble," Tamara yells at her.

"We're just having a good time," Charla says. "A *real* good time."

"Sit down here and cool off for a minute," Aya tells her. Charla obeys and sits beside Aya and Gregg.

About fifteen minutes later, Tamara notices that Monique and Keith are walking toward the exit. He has his arm around her and she is walking like she is nearly passed-out drunk. "I know that girl is not going home with a complete stranger," Tamara yells to Aya.

"Leave her alone," Charla shouts to them. "She's having the time of her life."

Before Tamara and Aya can get through the crowd on the floor, Monique and Keith are gone. Tamara and Aya make it to the door only to find no trace of the couple in the parking lot. They call for Monique several times, but to no avail. They make their way back to the table to find Jennifer and another guy sitting with Charla and Antonio.

"We couldn't find them," Aya says. "He must have been parked up close."

"She'll be OK," says Tamara. "She's done this before."

As the group stands to go to the dance floor, Jennifer notices something on the table. "What's this?" she asks.

Tamara and Aya move closer to examine the small bottle in her hand. "It was sitting here beside our drinks."

Case Study Analysis

Name _____ Date _____

Class _____ Section _____

1. What are the **facts** you KNOW about the case?
_____
_____
_____

2. What are some **logical assumptions** you can make about the case?
_____
_____
_____

3. What are the **problems** involved in the case as you see it?
_____
_____
_____

4. What is the **root problem** (the main issue)?
_____
_____

5. What do you estimate is the **cause of the root problem**?
_____
_____

6. What are the **reasons** that the root problem exists?
_____
_____
_____

7. What is (are) the **solution(s)** to the problem?
_____
_____
_____

8. Are there any **moral and/or ethical considerations** to your solution?

_____

_____

_____

9. What are the **consequences** of your solution?

_____

_____

_____

10. What are the **"real-world" implications** for this case?

_____

_____

_____

11. How will the **lives** of the people in the case study **be changed** because of your proposed solution?

_____

_____

_____

12. Where are some **areas on campus** that one could get help with the problems associated with this case?

_____

_____

_____

13. Where are some **areas beyond the campus** that one could get help with the problems associated with this case?

_____

_____

_____

14. What **personal advice** would you give to Monique, Charla, and the gang?

_____

_____

_____

Staying Connected

AT A GLANCE

Some would argue that the primary purpose of higher education is to educate citizens who can, and will, function well in a civilized world. Others would argue that while academics are important and necessary, the extracurricular events in college are just as important. Staying connected to your academics while enjoying the benefits of club, cultural, sporting, and entertainment events is a delicate balancing act.

10

At a Glance

CASE 1   Cutting the Apron Strings

Michael is nervous about attending an Ivy League school in the East. Although he is pleased to have been accepted, he now wonders if he will fit in and if he will be able to keep the grades required for his scholarship. He is very close to his family and is concerned about making it without their daily support. He especially depends on his dad and has a hard time imagining how he will get along without his advice. Does father know best?

CASE 2   The Big Mac Attack

John and three of his friends have been together since first grade. They have literally grown up together. Their summers have been spent playing baseball; they have been Boy Scouts in the same pack; they have grown up and dated together. For the first time, they are about to go their separate ways as they all prepare to go to college or to work. They face life without one another with apprehension. Is this the end of the Big Mac?

CASE 3   Connected on Campus

Leo is a straight-A student. He is majoring in Political Science with hopes of becoming a lawyer. He is deadly serious about his classes and his grades. When he discovers that one class requires him to join a club and another class requires him to miss several classes to go on two field trips, he is less than amused. Will his grades suffer because of his refusal to participate in extracurricular activities?

Cutting the Apron Strings

Michael arrives on campus at the highly respected Ivy League school with many questions rolling around in his mind. "Will I fit in?" "Will I be able to cut it?" "Is everyone else rich?" "Do I have the right clothes?" "Should I join a fraternity?" "What will my roommate be like?" "Am I really prepared for the academic rigor expected in my major?" "Can I make the grades required for law school?" "How will I manage without my family?"

His parents accompany him from Santa Fe because they have always supported him in everything he has done. They are a very close family, and Mike already wonders how he can handle all the things they have helped him with until now. His dad has always been his best friend, and he knows he will miss him very much. As they depart for home, Michael feels very lost and alone.

His suitemates represent a cross section of the country—one is from Atlanta, another from San Francisco, another from New York, and one from a small midwestern town in Iowa. While they are all nice enough, he knows very little about any of them and feels very lonely. They all seem so sophisticated and confident. He wishes he had his dad to talk to and is tempted to call him, but he remembers that his parents won't be back home until very late. He has a long sleepless night and is very homesick. He even misses his little sister, who has always been such a pain, always nosing into his business and trying to be a part of what he is doing. He must be really homesick to miss her!

The next day after orientation, he explores the city, which is so cosmopolitan and different from anything he has ever known. As he wanders through the shops and museums, he realizes that his background is very different. He pays attention to the students' dress on campus and thinks that his wardrobe needs some work if he is going to fit in here. "I wonder if there is anyone else like me on this entire campus? I need someone to talk to about all this, but I can't be a baby and call home every day."

Classes begin the next day. He is immediately stunned with the amount of work expected. He talks to people around him, but he doesn't really connect with anyone. They all seem so capable of handling everything. That afternoon, he decides to call his dad at work.

His dad immediately asks, "Is anything wrong? I didn't expect to hear from you for a while. How are things going?"

"Well, Dad, I'm fine. Pretty overwhelmed with the amount of work I have to get done, but I guess I expected that."

"How do you like your roommates?"

"They're nice guys." Michael replies. "I think they will be fine. They are different and from all over the country so they take a little getting used to, but I feel sure it will work out. I just wanted to tell you I'm doing OK."

That night, the guys decide to go out to a local hangout, so Michael, wanting to fit in, goes along. They discuss IDs and Michael confesses that he is only 17 and doesn't have a legal ID. One of his roommates says, "Oh, that's no problem. I've got several. You can use one of them. Let's find one that looks like you. Let's get an ID for the baby," he laughs. This worries Michael, but he wants to fit in so he takes the ID and is able to enter the bar. Michael has never been a big drinker, but he is obviously with a group that is. Soon they are laughing and talking boisterously while they play pool. Trying to fit in, Michael drinks way more than he is accustomed to. Soon, he finds himself in the bathroom throwing up. "What's the matter, Mikey," asks his roommate from New York. "Can't cut it?" He laughs and leaves Michael in the bathroom. Obviously, if he gets in trouble by drinking too much, he can't count on this group to care.

When he goes outside, all the guys jump on him and tease him about his inability to drink. Michael is embarrassed, but he is also confused. He and his dad have talked a lot about drinking. His mom and dad have made it very clear that they expect him to attend class, to manage his finances responsibly, and to schedule more study time than social time. They have emphatically emphasized the need not to drink too much and the dangers associated with college kids who drink too much.

He remembers his high school counselor's class on drinking and responsibility at college. The facts had impressed him and made him determined not to be a statistic. His counselor said, "Alcohol is related to 29 percent of dropouts, 38 percent of academic failures, 64 percent of violent behaviors, 66 percent of unsafe sexual practices, and 75 percent of acquaintance rapes." Michael has come to college determined to be responsible because he is focused on his goal of becoming a lawyer. He knows he has to have very good grades to get in a reputable law school.

When they leave the bar, Jeff, from New York, is driving and is very drunk. Michael knows his father would be very worried and upset with him if he could see him now. Miraculously, they make it back to their suite, where Michael is sick the rest of the evening. Roger, from San Francisco, passes out on the bathroom floor.

The next day, Michael leaves early for class. He is tired, and his head is throbbing from too much alcohol. He can't concentrate on the professors' lectures. "No wonder alcohol is related to academic failure," he thinks.

Early in the afternoon, his dad calls. "Just checking on you to see how things are going." Michael lies to his father and tells him that everything is fine. "I'm having a blast." "How's the party scene?" his dad asks. Again, Michael lies because he doesn't want to worry his father. "Not much time for that, Dad. It's really tough here, and I'm trying to keep up." He really wants to tell his dad the truth and seek his advice, but he doesn't want his mom and dad worried about him.

When he checks his mail that afternoon, he finds a big box of home-made cookies from his grandmother along with a very nice note. She tells him how proud she is of him for "going to that fancy school" and how much she loves him and believes in him. Tears come to his eyes because he misses his family so much. But he quickly recovers and goes back to his room.

That night his suitemates announce that they are going drinking again. Michael wants to get along with his roommates, but he also wants to pass his classes. And the truth is, he really doesn't want to go drinking. So he begs off by telling them he has to study. "Study! You just got here. Why don't you lighten up and have some fun? You can study later." He stands his ground and tells them he is going to stay in. Jeff taunts him. "You are such a wuss. Why did you come to college anyway? To sit around in your room and be a bookworm?"

As they exit laughing and poking fun at him, Michael feels very alone and lost. He thinks about his family and wishes he were with them.

Case Study Analysis

Name _____ Date _____

Class _____ Section _____

1. What are the **facts** you KNOW about the case?

_____

_____

_____

2. What are some **logical assumptions** you can make about the case?

_____

_____

_____

3. What are the **problems** involved in the case as you see it?

_____

_____

_____

_____

4. What is the **root problem** (the main issue)?

_____

_____

5. What do you estimate is the **cause of the root problem**?

_____

_____

6. What are the **reasons** that the root problem exists?

_____

_____

_____

7. What is (are) the **solution(s)** to the problem?

_____

_____

_____

174

8. Are there any **moral and/or ethical considerations** to your solution?

_____

_____

_____

9. What are the **consequences** of your solution?

_____

_____

_____

10. What are the **"real-world" implications** for this case?

_____

_____

_____

11. How will the **lives** of the people in the case study **be changed** because of your proposed solution?

_____

_____

_____

12. Where are some **areas on campus** that one could get help with the problems associated with this case?

_____

_____

_____

13. Where are some **areas beyond the campus** that one could get help with the problems associated with this case?

_____

_____

_____

14. What **personal advice** would you give to Michael?

_____

_____

_____

The Big Mac Attack

John and his friends are struggling with the fact that they are about to be separated for the first time since they were little boys. They always do everything together—baseball, Boy Scouts, dating, prom. You name it. If you see one, you see the others. John's girlfriend, BJ, often teases him that he loves his friends more than he loves her.

This fun-loving, sports-minded gang has earned a special name for their band of brothers. They formed a fearsome foursome on the football team's line that garnered them the name "the Big Mac Attack." This nickname has made them very popular in the neighborhood as well as at their school. When their team won the state championship, the Big Mac Attack was so popular that they could hardly walk down the halls at school.

But now that is about to end. Things will never be quite the same again, and they all feel the stress of learning to make it alone. Antonio is heading for Texas Tech on a football scholarship; Mario is going to the local community college to study welding; Francis is going to work with his father in his plumbing business; and John is headed for school in Virginia. The best student of the group by far, John hopes to study medicine.

John and BJ spend their last summer at home with these lifelong friends, going to movies, enjoying long, lazy days at the lake, and eating at local restaurants. It's as though they all know that things are about to be so different for each of them individually and for all of them collectively.

Not only is he losing his support group of guys, John is also having to give up his steady girlfriend. He and BJ have been together since eighth grade. Neither of them can imagine dating anyone else, although they have decided to date others. BJ is going to college in California on a full scholarship to study sports medicine. Her dream has always been to be a trainer for a college football team. She can hardly give up a full scholarship to go to school in Virginia with John. Anyway, they agree that they need to go away and find out if this is the real thing.

So John arrives on campus in Virginia without his support group, feeling a more than a little lost. As soon as he is settled, he calls BJ. She, too, is lonely and missing their group of friends. John wonders if this is going to work. He wonders what the rest of the Big Mac Attack is doing tonight.

Days go by, and John gradually settles into his new life. He is learning to like his roommate, although he is nothing like his friends from the Big Mac Attack. Douglas is actually very cosmopolitan and knows nothing about football. He doesn't even read the sports page! He has traveled all over the world and entertains John with stories of his travels. John has traveled very little in this country and has never been abroad. As they become friends, Douglas invites him to backpack across Europe with him the next summer. John feels a little guilty for wanting to do this, fearing what BJ would say if he took off for the summer when they are planning to be together. And how would Antonio, Mario, and Francis feel if he did not come home for the summer except for a few days?

It takes a while for John to find a girl he wants to ask out. After all, he has been with BJ so long that it seems awkward to even think about looking at another girl. Finally, he gets up the nerve to invite Carolyn from his English class to dinner and a movie. He calls BJ to tell her, but her roommate tells him that she is not in. "I think she is at the football game with Jerry." John's heart drops. He can't stand the thought of BJ being out with someone else even though he is about to do the same thing. But this is what they agreed on.

John takes Carolyn to a quiet bistro and actually finds her easy to talk to. She is pretty and sophisticated and very different from BJ. She is studying art history and plans to work in a museum in New York this summer. She talks about art and music and Broadway. She plans to live in New York when she graduates. "I can't imagine living anywhere else," she tells John. He feels a little insecure, but he finds himself fascinated with all she knows and talks about so easily. For the first time, he finds himself wishing he knew more about art and music. He decides to go to New York to a play as soon as he can save the money. The movie is a comedy, and he finds himself laughing easily with Carolyn. After the movie, they have a drink at a sports bar. He is surprised to learn that not only does she like football but she understands it. He has a hard time imagining that he has actually been on a date with someone other than BJ and has had a good time.

When he gets home after midnight, he calls BJ just to talk. He finds her in, and they catch up on what is happening in each of their lives. John tells BJ that he has had a date, and she tells him that she has been dating a guy named Jerry and that she has actually been out with him several times. John feels hurt, but he conceals his feelings.

"I love California, John. I feel so free and uninhibited here. It's so different from that little town we grew up in. I don't think I can ever go back there and stay. I've even been thinking about staying out here this summer and working. Why don't you come out and work too? We could have a great time." John doesn't tell her about Europe. That's a long way off. He realizes as he hangs up, though, that he and BJ are drifting apart. Things just don't feel the same.

John continues to call BJ and his friends when he can, but he realizes that his calls are less frequent than when he arrived. When they do talk, they seem to have less and less to talk about. John knows he is changing. His courses are making him more sophisticated, and his new friends are affecting him in very positive ways. He feels like a different person. What will he have in common with Mario and Francis other than the fact that they played football together and were part of the Big Mac Attack? He feels a sense of loss, but he knows he can't go back; in fact, he doesn't want to go back.

He thinks about Francis that night and wonders how he's doing in the plumbing business. John realizes that it's been two months since he has called Francis. Of all the Big Mac Attack group, Francis was the one he always talked to about his problems. Francis always seemed more mature than the rest of them.

John calls Francis and is glad to hear his voice. They talk about the plumbing business. Francis tells John, "Well, it's not very exciting, but it's a pretty good living. Dad is teaching me how to run the business so he can work less in a year or so." John feels sad for Francis because he's never going to have the same opportunities to grow and change that John is having.

"And I have some news. Sharon and I are getting married at Christmas. I want the Big Mac Attack to be my groomsmen. Mario will be there, but Antonio may not be able to come home because of football if they go to a bowl game. Hope you and BJ can make it." Married! John can't imagine wanting to get married right now, when he is just beginning to find out who he is.

John tells Francis, "I wouldn't miss it for the world!" He realizes that he and BJ haven't even talked about Christmas. It's been only two months, and already it seems that his old gang is falling apart. He feels homesick, yet he knows he doesn't belong there anymore.

Thinking he might relate more to Antonio, who is in college in Texas, he calls him to talk. Antonio sounds very much as he always has. He's doing well as a red-shirt freshman on the football team. The coach has high hopes for him, he says, and he loves college football. He's dating several girls, all "babes." "Same old Antonio," John smiles to himself. At least some things never change. But as he finishes talking to Antonio, he realizes that his life has moved so far beyond football and girls. He wants to taste all of what life offers—to travel, to feel comfortable in museums and on Broadway, to be at ease with classical music. College is changing him in ways he never imagined. He wonders if his friends and BJ will even relate to him when they are all home for Christmas.

Case Study Analysis

Name _____   Date _____

Class _____   Section _____

1. What are the **facts** you KNOW about the case?

_____

_____

_____

2. What are some **logical assumptions** you can make about the case?

_____

_____

_____

3. What are the **problems** involved in the case as you see it?

_____

_____

_____

4. What is the **root problem** (the main issue)?

_____

_____

5. What do you estimate is the **cause of the root problem**?

_____

_____

6. What are the **reasons** that the root problem exists?

_____

_____

_____

7. What is (are) the **solution(s)** to the problem?

_____

_____

_____

8. Are there any **moral and/or ethical considerations** to your solution?

_____

_____

_____

9. What are the **consequences** of your solution?

_____

_____

_____

10. What are the **"real-world" implications** for this case?

_____

_____

_____

11. How will the **lives** of the people in the case study **be changed** because of your proposed solution?

_____

_____

_____

12. Where are some **areas on campus** that one could get help with the problems associated with this case?

_____

_____

_____

13. Where are some **areas beyond the campus** that one could get help with the problems associated with this case?

_____

_____

_____

14. What **personal advice** would you give to John and his friends?

_____

_____

_____

Connected on Campus

Leo hears the alarm clock and reaches over to stop its annoying buzz. Today begins the second week of classes for him at Maryola University. Leo is majoring in Political Science with hopes of getting a master's degree in Criminal Justice and then completing his doctorate in Law. From the time Leo was a child, all he wanted was to be a criminal defense lawyer. Maryola is making this possible with two substantial scholarships and a work-study program.

Leo convinces his parents that he will do better in college if he lives alone and does not have to contend with a room-mate. His parents agree to pay the extra board if he maintains a 4.0 during his first year at Maryola. He is determined to do so at any cost.

In high school, Leo made straight A's and graduated vale-dictorian of his class. He is determined to maintain a 4.0 average as he moves through his degrees in college. "With a 4.0, Yale Law School is a certainty," he thinks. His plans are to concentrate solely on his classes, his political internship, and his preparation for the LSAT.

As Leo heads to class through the courtyard on Monday morning, members from every club, organization, student chapter, and fraternity greet him. They are passing out fly-ers and prizes, have balloons and streamers decorating their booths, and are recruiting heavily for new members. Leo smiles politely and declines the flyers and any opportunity to chat with an organization. "I've got to keep focused," he thinks. "No time to party, no time to socialize, and no time for clubs. Focus. Focus. Focus."

Each day after class, Leo stops by the Student Center for a quick lunch and then goes straight to the Law Library to study and prepare for future classes. He uses the Law Library because he wants to be around people who are studying law, who know law, and who are going into a law field as he is. When he needs a book on a topic from the main library, he stops by there first, checks out the book, and takes it to the Law Library to read it.

Leo dresses in a coat and tie every day. He notices early in the first week that the students who dress well are treated better and served more quickly in the Law Library, so he makes a conscious decision to begin to "act" like a lawyer and dress like a lawyer every day. He even goes to the local El Portal luggage store and charges a moderately priced briefcase so that he does not have to carry a backpack into the Law Library.

As midterm exams conclude, Leo has his perfect 4.0 average. He is car-rying an A in English 101, an A in the History of Politics, an A in

Introduction to Criminal Justice, an A in Algebra, an A in Chemistry, and an A in Maryola 101, his first-year orientation course. Leo is less than pleased, however, when he discovers that one of the requirements for the orientation course is that he must investigate and join at least one campus club or organization. When this is announced in class, Leo makes an appointment to speak with his professor about the requirement.

"I simply don't have time to join a worthless club," he tells the professor. "My studies are very important to me, and a club will just get in the way."

"Leo," the professor says, "I'm not forcing you to go to every meeting of every club on campus. I just want you to investigate one club that interests you and join that club so that you will meet people with similar interests."

"I don't need any people right now," Leo bemoans. "I study every afternoon and evening until 11:00. I study on the weekends, I study on holidays, and there is just no time to join a club."

"That is your prerogative," Dr. Miller says, "but you can't get an A in the class unless you meet this requirement and give your report on the club at the end of the semester."

"You mean that you will ruin my 4.0 if I don't join a club?" Leo asks angrily.

"No, I will not ruin your 4.0," Dr. Miller recants. "You will."

Leo leaves Dr. Miller's class in a foul mood. "How does he have the right to tell me what I need to do on my time off? This is just crazy," he thinks. "I'm trying to make something of my life, and he wants me to goof off at a 'baking club' meeting." He walks straight to the Law Library to try to study for an upcoming Criminal Justice exam. He is unable to study because he is so angry.

Later in the week, Leo enters his English 101 class. He enjoys the class because the professor, Dr. Howard, allows students to choose their own topics for writing. Leo always chooses a law-related topic. He is now writing an essay on corporal punishment and its effect on society. However, on this day, Leo gets another blow to his well-planned study schedule.

Dr. Howard enters the room and begins to talk about an upcoming field trip. "Everyone is required to attend one of two field trips I've scheduled in the next three weeks. I've prepared an Excused Absence Field Trip Slip for each of you, and you need only fill in the date of your absence from other classes, make copies of it, and give it to your professors."

"Miss my classes," Leo thinks. "That's not going to happen." Leo raises his hand and asks for more details about the field trips. "Exactly where will we be going and what do you expect us to gain from these trips?" he asks.

"One of the field trips will involve a poetry reading and discussion afterward with a popular, well-published poet," Dr. Howard explains. "I expect this field trip to expose you to the life of a poet in America and help you understand and appreciate poetry more."

"And the second trip?" Leo asks.

"The second trip will be to our local newspaper office, the *Free Journal*. There, you will meet with two feature writers and learn about their day and how they create stories for the paper."

Leo's mind is filled with confusion, and he is pretty upset. He does not say any more in class, but on the way to his room, he is disgusted with field trips and clubs and people who want to take him away from his classes. "All I want is an education," he thinks. "I don't want any of this silly field-trippy, clubby business. If they think I'm going to miss a class or study time in the Law Library for this, they have another thing coming!"

Case Study Analysis

Name _____ Date _____

Class _____ Section _____

1. What are the **facts** you KNOW about the case?

_____

_____

2. What are some **logical assumptions** you can make about the case?

_____

_____

_____

3. What are the **problems** involved in the case as you see it?

_____

_____

_____

4. What is the **root problem** (the main issue)?

_____

_____

5. What do you estimate is the **cause of the root problem**?

_____

_____

6. What are the **reasons** that the root problem exists?

_____

_____

_____

7. What is (are) the **solution(s)** to the problem?

_____

_____

_____

8. Are there any **moral and/or ethical considerations** to your solution?

_____
_____
_____

9. What are the **consequences** of your solution?

_____
_____
_____

10. What are the "real-world" implications for this case?

_____
_____
_____

11. How will the **lives** of the people in the case study **be changed** because of your proposed solution?

_____
_____
_____

12. Where are some **areas on campus** that one could get help with the problems associated with this case?

_____
_____
_____

13. Where are some **areas beyond the campus** that one could get help with the problems associated with this case?

_____
_____
_____

14. What **personal advice** would you give to Leo?

_____
_____
_____

Personal Responsibility

hardly wait to get away from home so she can pursue her loves with-
our parental supervision. She never knew a letter of the alphabet
could be so much trouble.

AT A GLANCE

Parents in the 1950s and 1960s were concerned about sex, drugs, and rock
and roll. Today, little has changed. Parents, teachers, counselors, and friends
concern themselves with the well-being of those they love.
Personal responsibility, however, involves making a
commitment to ourselves to care for "us" as much as
we care for others. Personal responsibility means
that we take stock of who we are and what we have
to offer to others, and that we act accordingly.

CASE 1   Out on a Binge

Scott has a drinking problem that he is trying to control. He promises his parents that he will not drink at college, and they trust him since he has been in a program to help him stop drinking. He meets Winston and Chris, who love to party but who agree to help him control his drinking. One night at a party, Winston and Chris fail to keep their promise. It that what friends are for?

CASE 2   Sins of the Parents

Levia comes to college every day looking worn out. She has told her friend Suzanna that her boyfriend keeps her out late. One day in desperation, Levia confides to Suzanna that she has not had a boyfriend in over a year and that she is not sleeping at home because of her parents' crack parties. Will she have to become the parent?

CASE 3   A, B, C, D, E Feels So Good

Amanda has long dreamed of going to nursing school, and the day has finally arrived. In addition to enjoying taking care of people, Amanda likes to party. She is into alternative rock music. She can hardly wait to get away from home so she can pursue her loves without parental supervision. She never knew a letter of the alphabet could be so much trouble.

Out on a Binge

Scott is determined to make his college experience better than his high school experience. He intentionally chooses a college hundreds of miles from home so that he can have a "fresh start" away from anyone who knows him. Because of some problems, he was not very popular in high school, but he is determined that college will be better. "If I can just make a few new friends," he thinks, "life will improve."

As Scott begins orientation activities the week before classes start, he meets Winston Courter and Chris Henderson. They hit it off immediately and make plans to meet later in the evening for pizza at a local pub near the campus. "Finally," Scott thinks, "people who don't know me and don't expect anything out of me. I can have a fresh start."

Scott, Winston, and Chris meet at 7:00 P.M. They exchange stories, talk about their families and friends back home, and reveal their dreams for the future. When they are finished with their pizza, Wilson suggests that they come back to his apartment to talk more and have some beer.

"Where'd you get beer, man?" Scott asks. "You're not 21, are you?"

"No, I'm not 21," Wilson laughs. "But my Texas ID says I am. Don't I look 21 to you?"

Scott is getting a little nervous because he does not need to have this in his life at the moment. He politely declines and asks jokingly if he can have a rain check.

"Come on, man," Chris begs. "It's free beer."

"Yeah, dude. It doesn't come along often," Winston says.

"Nah," Scott says, "I have an 8:00 A.M. class tomorrow. I've still got to do some reading for class."

"Next time, dude."

Scott goes back to his room and thinks about how close he came to just saying yes and having a drink with his new friends. "I can't let this happen again," he thinks to himself. "My parents trusted me to come here, and I've got to stick to my promise not to start drinking again." Scott sits on the side of the bed thinking about all of the times he worried his parents by getting drunk and staying out until all hours of the morning. "I just can't do it again."

On Friday, Scott runs into Winston and Chris at the Student Center. They sit together for a quick lunch before their next class. "So," Winston says, "how about doing something tonight?"

"That's cool with me," Chris says. "How about you, Scott?"

"What have you got in mind?" Scott asks.

"Some of the gang from my design class is meeting at Railroads. We can meet them there for a couple of drinks and then hit the bowling alley or catch a movie. That new Jackie Chan flick starts tonight."

"I'm in," Chris says. "You coming, Scott?"

"Tell me what time the movie starts, and I'll meet you guys there," Scott says.

"Come on, dude, you keep blowing us off. What gives?" Winston asks.

"I'm not blowing you guys off. I just may not be able to make it out early," Scott explains.

"There's more than that going on here, man. We're not blind," Chris states.

Scott begins to feel his face turn red and knows that he needs to explain to his new buddies that he can't be around a lot of booze right now. He explains to them that he has a drinking problem and that he is trying to stay clear of situations where alcohol might be a problem.

"That's cool," Winston says. "How much were you drinking in high school?"

"A lot, man," Scott answers. "A lot. Every day."

"Well, you're not drinking now, are you?" Chris asks.

"No. I have not had a drink in two months and three days," Scott explains.

"Well, I'll tell you what," Winston says. "Come with us tonight, and we'll make sure you don't drink. If you do, we'll stop you before you drink too much. How's that?"

"I don't know about that," Scott says shyly. "I just need to keep my promise to my parents that I won't do like I did in high school."

Later that evening, Winston and Chris stop by to pick up Scott to go to Railroads.

"How do you guys plan to get us into this place and how do you plan to get a beer in public?" Scott asks.

Chris and Winston laugh as they both pop out their fake IDs. "Remember this? You hang with us, man. We'll take care of you," Winston says.

They enter Railroads with no trouble at all. The bar is known for its lax standards on entrance. Once inside, Winston and Chris head for the bar and order two drafts and a diet cola. They stand around and talk for a while until the other students show up. After an hour, the gang is having a good time, Scott included. They all get along and have a pool tournament going. Winston has won two games, and Scott is up in the next game. Things are going well.

Winston, Chris, and most of the other students, some older, have been drinking steadily since they arrived. Scott leans over to Chris and asks, "Can you get me one of those, man," referring to the beer in Chris's hand.

"Sure, dude," Chris says, "but are you sure you wanna do this?"

"It's just one beer," Scott says. "I just need to know that I can have a few drinks and not go crazy."

"Well, who am I to mess around with a scientific experiment?" Chris asks as he heads for the bar. He returns with two full mugs of beer. Chris makes a toast, and they down half the beers in one chug.

Before the evening is over, all three guys are wasted. Scott is not as drunk as Chris and Winston, but he is drunk. They drink and play pool and sing to the jukebox until early in the morning, when they hitch a ride back to the college with another student.

Scott does not wake up until after 2:00 on Saturday. His head is hurting, and he is depressed that he let himself get so wasted. But in the back of his mind, he thinks, "I did have a great time. Now, I just have to lay off the booze until next weekend. I can do this."

As the next week progresses, Scott does not drink a single alcoholic beverage. However, on Wednesday, Winston and Chris invite him to a party on Friday night at a friend's house. Scott gladly agrees to attend. At the party, he paces himself for the first hour, but by 11:00 P.M., he has had six or seven beers. The crowd is wild and the music is great. He is having a great time getting to know new people.

Again, Scott sleeps past 2:00 on Saturday. When he wakes up, he has another hangover but feels proud that he made it a whole week and did not drink. "I've got this licked," he says to himself. "There is no problem if I only drink once a week on the weekend. I'm doing OK."

Case Study Analysis

Name _____ Date _____

Class _____ Section _____

1. What are the **facts** you KNOW about the case?

   _____

   _____

2. What are some **logical assumptions** you can make about the case?

   _____

   _____

3. What are the **problems** involved in the case as you see it?

   _____

   _____

   _____

4. What is the **root problem** (the main issue)?

   _____

   _____

5. What do you estimate is the **cause of the root problem**?

   _____

   _____

6. What are the **reasons** that the root problem exists?

   _____

   _____

   _____

7. What is (are) the **solution(s)** to the problem?

   _____

   _____

   _____

8. Are there any **moral and/or ethical considerations** to your solution?

_____

_____

_____

9. What are the **consequences** of your solution?

_____

_____

_____

10. What are the **"real-world" implications** for this case?

_____

_____

_____

11. How will the **lives of the people in the case study be changed** because of your proposed solution?

_____

_____

_____

12. Where are some **areas on campus** that one could get help with the problems associated with this case?

_____

_____

_____

13. Where are some **areas beyond the campus** that one could get help with the problems associated with this case?

_____

_____

_____

14. What **personal advice** would you give to Scott?

_____

_____

_____

Sins of the Parents

Levia enters class groggy and tired from the night before. She struggles to stay awake during the lecture. After class, she meets up with Suzanna, a friend from class. They decide to go to the Student Center for a cup of coffee. "Well, you were a little late today," Suzanna says. "Looks like you had a rough night. Who was he?" Levia can't answer because she knows that with one word the tears will come. She sits silently until Suzanna puts her hand on her shoulder and asks, "What's wrong, girl? Did someone hurt you?"

Levia's emotions are so close to the edge that she can feel the tears begin to stream down her face. "It's my parents," she answers. "I've got to get the hell out of that house. They are driving me crazy."

"What's wrong?" Suzanna asks. "Are they on your case about dating or coming in late?"

"Suzanna, I haven't had a date in over a year," Levia says.

"What are you talking about? You date two or three times a week. You told me so. You said that your boyfriend keeps you out late and that is why you get to class so late and look so groggy," Suzanna reminds her.

"It's all a lie," Levia says through the tears. "I get to school late because my parents are up to 3:00 and 4:00 in the morning having crack parties. I've got to do something before I get killed or arrested."

"CRACK PARTIES!" Suzanna says in shock. "Your parents do crack?"

"They've been on crack so long I don't even know who they are when they are not high. When they are not on crack, they are high on alcohol or pot. I just can't go on like this," she says.

"Why haven't you told me?" Suzanna asks.

"Would you tell people that your parents keep you up at night because their 'friends' come over at 11:00 P.M. and do crack until they all pass out on the living room floor?" Levia questions. "I'm so embarrassed and humiliated and sickened over the whole thing that I can't even think straight anymore. My father lost his job three months ago, my mom hasn't worked in two years, and when they found out that I got $200 back from my financial aid check, my father went into my purse and stole the money. I don't have anything," she says through the tears streaming down her face.

"I'm sorry," Suzanna says. "I don't know what else to say."

"There is nothing to say. I've got to quit school and find me a place to live before I wind up dead or raped in my own bedroom."

They stand and begin to walk toward the Academic Center. "There isn't any need for me to go to this class," Levia says. "I just need to go drop all of this and start looking for a place to live."

"Can you hold on for just a while longer?" Suzanna asks. "Maybe we can find help and you won't have to drop out."

"I don't think there is any help for people like me," Levia says. "How many students here deal with drug- and alcohol-addicted parents?"

"Have you talked to your parents about what they're doing to you? Have you let them know how much pain they are causing?"

"They don't care about anything but their next high. . . . The man stole the money for my college textbooks. Does that tell you how concerned they are about me?"

"This is a crazy question, but I'm going to ask it anyway. Have you considered turning them into the police? Have you told them that you are going to do it?"

"If I said that to my father, he'd put a gun to my head and pull the trigger. He would literally kill me now or when he got out of prison," Levia says.

"He wouldn't actually do that," Suzanna says. "You're his child."

"He told me about a year ago that if I ever brought another person to our house that we'd both be found in a shallow grave under the house. Now what does that tell you?"

"Jeez," Suzanna says. "This is the worst thing I've ever heard. But after this class, we're going to find someone to help us."

During class, Levia's mind is filled with thoughts of despair, fear, anger, and even suicide. She can't think her way through the situation. She can't move beyond the fear to decide what is right and what should be done. Her only joy is that, now, one other person knows the truth. She does not feel so alone. She has Suzanna to talk to about the entire mess. That is the only bright spot that has come into her life in months.

After class, Suzanna tells Levia that she has thought of a solution to the problem. Levia is elated to have another perspective on the situation. "This is what we're gonna do," Suzanna says. "You're not going to call the police. I'm going to pretend that I am a neighbor and that I am tired of the noise and constant 'in-and-out' action at your house. This way, they won't think that you called the police. What do you think about that?" Suzanna asks.

"Girl, did you not listen to anything I said. That man will kill me. He will know that I had something to do with it, and he'll come after me with guns loaded. No! There will be no police calling," Levia says sharply.

"But the police will tell them that the neighbors called," Suzanna says.

"I said no. This is my life, and if that is the only way out, I'll just drop out of college and find me a job and a cheap apartment. I don't want to die over this," Levia says.

"If you don't do something soon," Suzanna pleads, "you might be dead anyway."

As Suzanna drives home, she is consumed with thoughts about Levia. She is worried about her home situation, her stress level, her studies, and her life. She is tempted to call the police herself and report Levia's parents but knows that Levia's life could be in danger if she does call. She wants to talk to her own parents about the whole thing, but she thinks that the fewer people who know, the better. She even considered talking to a counselor at the college about Levia's situation. She is scared for her good friend.

When she gets home, she decides to tell her mother a little about the situation and pretend that it is an example used in a textbook in her psychology class. She explains that a student's parents are drug and alcohol addicts and that the student's life is in jeopardy. She asks her mother's advice about the "fictitious" situation.

"I have to say that I would contact the authorities and let them handle it," Suzanna's mother states firmly. "That situation is too deep for anyone but the police."

Suzanna eats her dinner and goes to her room. She closes the door, walks over to her desk, pulls out the phone book, looks up a number, picks up the phone, and pauses to take a deep breath.

Case Study Analysis

Name _____   Date _____

Class _____   Section _____

1. What are the **facts** you KNOW about the case?

_____

_____

_____

2. What are some **logical assumptions** you can make about the case?

_____

_____

_____

3. What are the **problems** involved in the case as you see it?

_____

_____

_____

4. What is the **root problem** (the main issue)?

_____

_____

5. What do you estimate is the **cause of the root problem**?

_____

_____

6. What are the **reasons** that the root problem exists?

_____

_____

_____

7. What is (are) the **solution(s)** to the problem?

_____

_____

_____

8. Are there any **moral and/or ethical considerations** to your solution?

_____

_____

_____

9. What are the **consequences** of your solution?

_____

_____

_____

10. What are the **"real-world" implications** for this case?

_____

_____

_____

11. How will the **lives** of the people in the case study **be changed** because of your proposed solution?

_____

_____

_____

12. Where are some **areas on campus** that one could get help with the problems associated with this case?

_____

_____

_____

13. Where are some **areas beyond the campus** that one could get help with the problems associated with this case?

_____

_____

_____

14. What **personal advice** would you give to Levia?

_____

_____

_____

A, B, C, D, E Feels So Good

Amanda can hardly believe that the day has finally come for her to leave for college. She has chosen a small four-year college in Illinois that is recognized for having a good nursing program. She has dreamed of becoming a nurse since she was a little girl. She is equally excited about getting away from home so she can more openly pursue her love of alternative rock music. Amanda's friends understand her desire to wear a brow ring and to have her navel pierced. Her father, on the other hand, is ultra-conservative and will not allow her to attend her favorite bands' concerts, nor will he allow her to wear her brow ring. To pursue her interests, she has had to sneak around and disobey her father. She is so happy to finally be able to be her own boss.

In spite of her extracurricular activities, Amanda has always been an excellent student. She knows that the nursing curriculum is difficult and that she must take several upper-level science courses. From the beginning, she applies herself and her grades are good. As soon as she is settled, she volunteers at one of the local hospitals and begins accumulating hours that will help her when she applies for summer positions.

The nurses like her attitude and give her more and more responsibilities as they begin to trust her. She is wise enough to leave her brow ring at home and not to discuss her interests in alternative music. She can't imagine the nursing staff at this hospital understanding her other life.

Amanda is disappointed that no alternative rock bands have played anywhere near her college campus. Finally, she reads in the local paper that one of her favorite bands is coming to Chicago, only two hours away. Amanda talks to her friends and gathers a group interested in going with her to hear them play on a Saturday a month away. She is so excited!

The day of the concert, Amanda takes special pains to get her hair dyed a bright fuchsia color. She inserts her brow ring and navel ring and wears her collar with the spikes. She will fit in perfectly with this audience. Even her new friends who are into alternative rock are a little taken back with her different appearance.

After they arrive, Amanda and her new friends smoke marijuana in the parking lot before going in. Amanda has experimented with marijuana before but has never been willing to use hard drugs. As they enter the coliseum where the show is being staged, Amanda feels that she is with her own kind. Their dress reflects her tastes, and they love her kind of music. She feels free and alive!

At intermission, one of her friends passes around pills to the entire group. "This will make the next half even more exciting. Try these beans." Amanda has never tried any kind of pills, but after all, she is a college student now, and "This is part of the experience," she thinks. "And anyway, it's just this once. I won't make a habit of this." During the concert, Amanda and her friends are hyper-excitable; two of them appear to be very nervous, and one complains of itching. Their sense of enjoyment increases significantly.

After the concert, Brad suggests that they all go to a nightclub known for its mash pit and raves. Feeling very high, they all agree and spend the rest of the evening dancing, high on pills and booze. Although Amanda normally does not smoke, she smokes several cigarettes during the evening.

When they return to campus, Amanda tells her roommate what a great time they have had and how Brad introduced her to pills known as "beans." "Talk about a high. We had a blast!" Her roommate is concerned at Amanda's behavior. Her outside interests just do not seem to match her career ambitions. She notices that Amanda has bruises on her arms and legs and wonders if this is a result of the mash pit she talked about. "I hope Amanda knows what she is doing," she thinks.

Amanda goes to class and gets back an exam on which she made an A. Her professor, Dr. Simkins, calls her aside and tells her how much the nurses at University Hospital like her and how complimentary they are of her work and of her attitude. "You are going to be a great nurse," says Dr. Simkins. "I look forward to working with you during the next four years. Once in a while someone comes along who is just meant to be a nurse, and you are one of them. You might even want to consider graduate school after you get experience. We need good professors."

Amanda is elated that things are working out just as she had planned. She can hardly wait to get to work and see her friends and patients at the hospital. She has become especially attached to an elderly woman, Mrs. Bryan, who rarely has any visitors. Amanda has given her special attention, and the old woman has grown very fond of her. She tells one of the nurses that she is considering paying for Amanda's tuition because she doesn't have any grandchildren and Amanda has filled a special need for her. "I'd like to help her and follow her career. She is a very impressive young woman."

As Amanda goes about her work at the hospital that afternoon, she can hardly believe her good fortune. As she comes out of Mrs. Bryan's room, the head nurse calls her over to the desk. "Amanda, we are required to conduct random drug testing for all our volunteers and interns. I'd like to do your test now. By the way, we are introducing a new test in our series that requires a strand of hair." Amanda is surprised and a little concerned. Will the marijuana show up on the test? What was that pill that Brad had passed around? Why a strand of hair? She wishes that she knew more about the test and what they are looking for.

During the next two days, the drug test crosses Amanda's mind frequently. Hopefully, everything was out of her system before they tested her. Two days after the test, she is scheduled to work at the hospital again. The head nurse approaches her as soon as she arrives. "Amanda, will you come in my office, please? I need to talk to you." Amanda's heart is beating faster because she is afraid of what the test might have shown.

The head nurse has a hurt and puzzled look on her face. "Amanda, I have some very bad news, and I am really shocked that I have to tell you, of all people, this news. The results of your drug test are positive for marijuana, ecstasy, and tobacco." "Ecstasy," Amanda thinks. "I had no idea. And tobacco. I didn't even know they could test for tobacco."

The head nurse explained to Amanda that the old test did not test for ecstasy. "In the past, the fact that you had used this drug very recently would not have been disclosed. The tobacco test is new also." Amanda is numb. This news has stunned her. How could she have been so careless and stupid! She has jeopardized her dreams.

"Amanda, I hate to have to tell you this because we all love you, but I can't keep you on as a volunteer at the hospital. Our regulations are very strict. I'll also have to report the results of your test to your college and to the School of Nursing. I don't know what they will do with the results of this test, but I can tell you that most public health programs will not allow students who have positive drug tests to be enrolled. As you know, the clinical component of your degree is crucial. No hospital in this area is going to accept you until you have a clean drug record for at least two years. I'm going to have to ask you to get your things and leave the hospital."

Case Study Analysis

Name _____ Date _____

Class _____ Section _____

1. What are the **facts** you KNOW about the case?

_____

_____

_____

2. What are some **logical assumptions** you can make about the case?

_____

_____

_____

3. What are the **problems** involved in the case as you see it?

_____

_____

_____

4. What is the **root problem** (the main issue)?

_____

_____

_____

5. What do you estimate is the **cause of the root problem**?

_____

_____

6. What are the **reasons** that the root problem exists?

_____

_____

_____

7. What is (are) the **solution(s)** to the problem?

_____

_____

_____

8. Are there any **moral and/or ethical considerations** to your solution?

_____

_____

_____

9. What are the **consequences** of your solution?

_____

_____

_____

10. What are the "**real-world**" **implications** for this case?

_____

_____

_____

11. How will the **lives** of the people in the case study **be changed** because of your proposed solution?

_____

_____

_____

12. Where are some **areas on campus** that one could get help with the problems associated with this case?

_____

_____

_____

13. Where are some **areas beyond the campus** that one could get help with the problems associated with this case?

_____

_____

_____

14. What **personal advice** would you give to Amanda?

_____

_____

_____

CHAPTER 12

Dealing with Difficult People

AT A GLANCE

A sad part of life is that we must interact with people who are mean, empty, rude, and downright awful. The great part of life is that we don't encounter them every day. Many of the experiences you have and the classes that you take in college will help you deal with difficult people. One key way to survive an unhealthy, mean-spirited attack is to not allow oneself to be taken into the abyss with the mean person. It is also one of life's hardest lessons.

12

205

CASE 1   The Nutty Professor

Donna, Linwood, and Tony are all enrolled in a statistics course that they later find out has the reputation of being the most difficult course on campus. Dr. Whann is also considered the hardest, most unapproachable professor on campus. When Donna tries to meet with him, she discovers that a teaching assistant keeps his office hours, and that when Dr. Whann does show up, he will not speak with students without appointments. Will Dr. Whann get the best of the group?

CASE 2   Trouble in Music City

Jody is excited about finally starting her college career. She worked two years after high school to save money for college. Her father died when she was a small child, and she has always known she would have to educate herself because her mother cannot afford to do it. Jody views the necessity to work as an opportunity to have a head start in her career. Will her hard work pay off?

CASE 3   Roommate from Hell

Jack arrives on campus from a small town outside St. Louis. Having gone to a small, conservative private high school, Jack has chosen a college that he feels matches the environment to which he is accustomed. His idea of college life is quickly marred within a few hours of his roommate's arrival on campus. Can hell be worse?

The Nutty Professor

Donna leaves Dr. Whann's class with a major headache. "I don't mean to be rude," she says to her classmate Linwood, "but that is the damnedest class I have ever had in my life. I can't understand half of what he is saying, and God forbid that you try to stop him to ask him a question. I'm just lost. I need to drop this class," she says.

"Wait a while longer," Linwood says. "It's bound to get better. It can't get any worse."

Little do they know how wrong that statement is. As the classes continue, things go from awful to atrocious. Dr. Whann's statistics class is known for being one of the hardest on campus, and he is considered one of the most demanding and unapproachable professors at the university. "Why didn't someone warn us at orientation?" Donna asks Linwood. "WHY????"

"Well, that's one of the drawbacks of being a first-year student," he says. "There is no one to ask."

"OK," Donna says at the study group, "what are we going to do about this? The man can't teach, he doesn't speak clearly, he keeps his back to us most of the class, he's never in his office during office hours, and he yells at you in class if you raise your hand. I've just had it with him. What are we going to do?"

"I think we should go to his department chair and complain," Wanda says.

"But what if he finds out that we are the ones who complained about him?" Linwood asks. "He could make it worse on us."

"WORSE!" Tony blares out. "How could it be worse? The man doesn't even care if we are dead or alive. He certainly doesn't care if we're learning or not."

The group is having a hard time with the difficult material and with a professor who seems intent on making the class as difficult as possible. English is not Dr. Whann's first language, he has never taken a class in teaching methodology, he has no patience for students who do not understand the material on the first attempt, he yells at students who answer incorrectly in class, and he ridicules those who dare raise their hands in class. He is constantly late for class, keeps his back to the students as he works at the board, has his graduate assistant keep office hours for him, and is indeed an unapproachable character.

"Maybe if we went to his office together," Linwood says, "he would see that there is more than one of us who is struggling. Maybe he would be kinder if he saw us together."

"Yeah, right," Donna jokes, "and he'll have pizza and soda there for us to wish us well." The group laughs together.

"So, what are we going to do?" Tony asks. "We're all failing this one class. We're not failing any other classes, so if we go to the chair, he has to understand that this is Dr. Whann's problem, not ours."

"Or he could say that this is just our attempt to get out of working," Linwood says.

"All I know is that I cannot fail this class," Donna says. "I've never failed a class in my life, and I'm not going to start now. I'm going to his office to ask for help. I'm going to give him one more try, and then I'm going higher."

"You go, girl," Judy jokes.

Donna goes to Dr. Whann's office during his office hours. As usual, he is not in the office. She questions his graduate assistant about his arrival time.

"I really don't know," he says. "He gets here when he gets here."

"Well, what time does he usually get here on Wednesdays?" Donna queries.

"He has a class in Beamme Hall at 1:00, and he usually comes to the office after that class," the assistant says.

"I'll be back at 2:00," she says.

At 2:00, Donna is waiting at the door for Dr. Whann. As she sees his petite form shuffle down the tiled hall, her heart begins to beat faster and she can feel herself getting short of breath. As he approaches his door, he does not even acknowledge her presence.

"Dr. Whann," she says gently. "May I have a moment of your time? I'm in your statistics class on Tuesdays and Thursdays."

"Office hours are not now," he says sharply.

"I know, sir, but I was here during your office hours and you were not here. . . . I mean you were not available," she says quietly, trying not to be offensive or to upset him.

"You come back during tomorrow hours," he says loudly.

"But, sir, I desperately need to speak with you about the assignment due in the morning. I just can't understand the formula."

"If you read book, you understand. You no read book, that why you stupid on issue," he says curtly.

"Excuse me, sir," she says candidly. "I did read the book and I even attended my study session. I need your help." She can feel herself getting angry now and tries to control her emotions and vocal tone.

"You read book like other student read book, you understand. You no read book, I not speak with you."

"The other students do not understand it either, Dr. Whann," she tries to explain.

"Oh, so now you know what everybody know, is that right?"

"No, sir," she tries to explain. "I just know that no one in my study group understands the formula either."

"Stupid people hang with stupid people," he says as he begins to shut the office door in her face.

"I am not a stupid person, Dr. Whann," she replies. "You're just not teaching us what you're supposed to be teaching. You're not helping us at all."

The door slams in her face. Donna is livid with anger. She can't believe that anyone could be so insensitive . . . especially a college professor. She gathers her belongings and walks toward the library, where the study group is waiting.

"So, how did it go?" Linwood asks.

"He slammed the door in my face," she states. "IN MY FACE!"

"He did not," Judy says jokingly.

"Slammed the door," Donna states bluntly. "It's personal now."

Case Study Analysis

Name _____ Date _____

Class _____ Section _____

1. What are the **facts** you KNOW about the case?

_____

_____

_____

2. What are some **logical assumptions** you can make about the case?

_____

_____

_____

_____

3. What are the **problems** involved in the case as you see it?

_____

_____

_____

4. What is the **root problem** (the main issue)?

_____

_____

5. What do you estimate is the **cause of the root problem**?

_____

_____

6. What are the **reasons** that the root problem exists?

_____

_____

_____

7. What is (are) the **solution(s)** to the problem?

_____

_____

_____

8. Are there any **moral and/or ethical considerations** to your solution?

_____

_____

9. What are the **consequences** of your solution?

_____

_____

_____

10. What are the **"real-world" implications** for this case?

_____

_____

_____

11. How will the **lives of the people in the case study be changed** because of your proposed solution?

_____

_____

12. Where are some **areas on campus** that one could get help with the problems associated with this case?

_____

_____

13. Where are some **areas beyond the campus** that one could get help with the problems associated with this case?

_____

_____

14. What **personal advice** would you give to Donna, Linwood, and the group?

_____

_____

Trouble in Music City

J Jody has selected a college in Nashville because she is also an amateur country singer and hopes to pursue her love of performing. Her goal is to get a job in a music business while she looks for a break. She has experience singing in local clubs back home, where people thought she was very good. She was often told that she should try to make it in country music.

Having worked two years after high school, she arrives on campus with enough money to make it through her first two years. She thinks she can use a combination of scholarships and part-time work to help her complete her baccalaureate degree without having to stop and work full-time. Therefore, she knows she has to find a good part-time job that pays as much as possible. In high school, Jody took every computer class available. In addition, the company she worked for paid for several computer certifications, so she has highly marketable skills that command good pay. She has planned carefully!

Jody has rented a small efficiency apartment. After unpacking her things and setting up her computer and printer, she goes online to search for a job. She begins her search with a music company. After searching through quite a few job postings that don't appeal to her, she finds an advertisement for a part-time computer operator at Warren Productions. She e-mails her application letter and attaches her resume.

The next day after classes, she is pleased to see that a Mrs. Hampton from Warren Productions has responded to her application and requested an interview. This sounds like a great job to Jody, and Mrs. Hampton seems very friendly when she calls for the interview. Jody can hardly wait for her interview. She has a good feeling about this company and the opportunities this position might offer. She dresses carefully in her dark suit, which she pressed the night before, and off she goes to her interview.

She is a little disappointed to find that Warren Productions is a fledgling company that employs only 12 people and operates from a rather small office building. Jody had visions of a big, plush sophisticated office associated with a high-powered music corporation. "Oh well, I might as well give it a try," she thinks.

In her usual punctual manner, Jody arrives early and waits for Mrs. Hampton to call her. While waiting, she chats with the office manager, who tells her about the company. It seems that Warren Productions is owned by a young man in his thirties who has his own band and manages several others. The operation seems rather informal. Jody talks about her background and shares the fact that she has several computer certifications. She senses that this is a little disturbing to the office manager, who admits that she has learned her computer skills "by hit and miss."

Trying to warm up to her, Jody also tells the office manager that she is a performer and hopes to break into country music. The office manager's attitude has become a little cool by the time Mrs. Hampton invites Jody into her office. Jody is puzzled by the change in her behavior.

Mrs. Hampton is a large, jovial woman whom Jody immediately likes. Her office and desk are a wreck, however, which bothers the neat and orderly Jody. "Maybe I can help her get better organized," Jody thinks.

The interview goes well. Mrs. Hampton is impressed with Jody's ambitious agenda to finish college while paying her own way. "I always wanted to go to college, but I have just had to make it the hard way. Experience is a hard teacher, but I've managed to do OK," Mrs. Hampton says. Jody agrees that experience is the very best teacher and senses that Mrs. Hampton, like the office manager, appears to have become a little distant.

However, Mrs. Hampton seems pleased that Jody has several computer courses and certifications and is complimentary. "You'll be the best qualified computer person in the building." Trying to act modest, Jody replies, "I doubt that, but you are very nice and encouraging." She does not discuss her music ambitions, deciding that this topic can be addressed later.

Mrs. Hampton hires Jody on the spot, telling her that she has interviewed several people and that she is by far the best qualified. Jody would prefer a little more money than she offers, but the fact that the owner has his own band appeals to her, so she accepts the job. Mrs. Hampton takes her around to meet the rest of the workforce, a part-time accountant, a promotions manager, and a booking manager, along with several people whose jobs are related to the production of recordings for the bands the company manages. Mrs. Hampton tells Jody that most of the people are "music star wannabees." "Personally, I gave up on that long ago," she says wistfully.

Jody comes to work excited and enthusiastic. The office manager assigns her a desk in a small cubicle in the back of the office. The computer she is given is old and outdated. "I can't run any of the software I am capable of using on this piece of junk," she thinks. As she was walking back to her cubicle earlier, she noticed that other staff people have much better equipment. "I hate to complain, but do you have a computer that is more updated? I can do so much more for the company if I can use my skills." The office manager, Maggie, responds, "You're the new kid on the block. You have to take what's left. Here's some work for you." Jody looks at it and moans to herself how long it will take on that outdated computer and how much better the document would look if she could use the right software. Why won't Maggie capitalize on her strengths? She just does not understand.

Later, the part-time accountant drops by to talk and comments on the "horse and buggy computer" that Maggie gave her. "Someone said she had it in for you and she must, judging by that dinosaur computer. We do have much better computers in our storage room. You might check it out." Jody is puzzled. What does Maggie have against her?

During the day, the young boss, Mack, comes in and walks back to meet Jody. Dressed in jeans and boots, he is handsome and charming. He tells her that he understands she is interested in singing country music. She responds that she is, excited that he has asked her about her interests. She wonders, "How did he know that?"

"We're rehearsing at my house tonight if you'd like to come by and let us take a look at your work." Jody can hardly believe her good fortune. "Oh, I'd love to!"

At Mack's house that evening, Jody thinks she has died and gone to heaven. His band is actually very good. They are all young and excited about their opportunities. After she sings "The Dance" for them, she can tell that she is a hit with them also. The band members applaud enthusiastically, and Mack says, "What do you think, guys? Should we take Jody on the road with us this weekend? We'll have to work hard to get ready to perform a few songs with her as lead vocalist, but I think this girl has got what it takes." Jody is thrilled. She can hardly wait to call her mother.

The next afternoon after class, she goes to work and Maggie is waiting for her. "Well, you are a smooth operator, aren't you?" Jody is stunned and inquires, "What do you mean?" "Well, it didn't take you long to kiss up to Mack. But don't be fooled by all that charm. He promised to help me get in the business too, but it never worked out."

Maggie continues, "I understand you've been complaining about your computer." Again, Jody is stunned. News travels fast in this company! "I just mentioned that I could do so much more for the company if I had a better computer." Maggie responds in a loud, shrill voice that can easily be heard by others. "Well, I'm in charge of this office, and you'll get a better computer if I say so." Mrs. Hampton interrupts their conversation and asks Jody to come to her office.

"Jody, I like you and I think you can be an asset to the company, but you are off to a bad start with Maggie and some of the other employees."

"I truly don't understand, Mrs. Hampton," Jody responds. "Obviously, Maggie doesn't like me, but I honestly don't know what I did to upset her."

"It's not just Maggie. You have to understand that some of these people have been around a long time hoping to get a break. Now, Mack walks in and offers you a chance the first time he meets you. They all know that he is going to let you perform with his band this weekend. You are young and pretty, as well as talented, and you will just have to deal with the fact that some people here are never going to like you. My advice is to do your job and stay out of their way. And just for your information, Mack has a reputation of loving the girls and leaving them. Be careful, or you'll get hurt."

Case Study Analysis

Name _____ Date _____

Class _____ Section _____

1. What are the **facts** you KNOW about the case?
   _____
   _____
   _____

2. What are some **logical assumptions** you can make about the case?
   _____
   _____
   _____

3. What are the **problems** involved in the case as you see it?
   _____
   _____
   _____

4. What is the **root problem** (the main issue)?
   _____

5. What do you estimate is the **cause of the root problem**?
   _____

6. What are the **reasons** that the root problem exists?
   _____
   _____
   _____

7. What is (are) the **solution(s)** to the problem?
   _____
   _____
   _____

8. Are there any **moral and/or ethical considerations** to your solution?

_____

_____

_____

9. What are the **consequences** of your solution?

_____

_____

_____

10. What are the **"real-world" implications** for this case?

_____

_____

_____

11. How will the **lives** of the people in the case study **be changed** because of your proposed solution?

_____

_____

_____

12. Where are some **areas on campus** that one could get help with the problems associated with this case?

_____

_____

_____

13. Where are some **areas beyond the campus** that one could get help with the problems associated with this case?

_____

_____

_____

14. What **personal advice** would you give to Jody?

_____

_____

_____

Roommate from Hell

Jack Todd arrives on campus at Sharpton College, a conservative, private liberal arts college in a small town. Having gone to a private school in Missouri, Jack believes that Sharpton will offer him an environment similar to the one he has been accustomed to and in which he will be more comfortable. His father is a minister, and Jack is leaning toward following in his dad's footsteps. He is considering becoming a youth minister, an occupation that will enable him to work with young people as a counselor as well as coach baseball for the Youth League.

Having received literature from Sharpton for several months, Jack already knows who his roommate will be. Bill Raymond is arriving from St. Louis a few hours after Jack. Although they have talked briefly on the phone, Jack knows very little about his future roommate except that he attended a large high school in St. Louis and that he is an athlete. Since Bill is attending Sharpton on an athletic scholarship, Jack hopes that their athletic interests will give them a common bond. He is, however, apprehensive and wonders if Bill will be a compatible roommate.

Since Bill is arriving late and Jack wants to get settled, he selects a bed and a closet and unpacks his clothes, sets up his computer, and begins to organize his desk. He has almost finished when Bill makes his entrance, girlfriend in tow. Bill is the consummate jock—big, gregarious, confident, and loud. He introduces his girlfriend, Mary, who is a sophomore at Sharpton. She and Bill have been dating for several years.

Bill immediately lets Jack know that the bed Jack has chosen is the one he wants. "I need to be by the window," he informs Jack. Wanting to get along, Jack agrees to swap. Bill proceeds to pile things around the room rather than unpacking in an orderly manner. He shoves Jack's clothes aside in the closet they share and takes up most of the space. Jack can tell after only a few minutes that his new roommate is a slob, and a rude one at that. This goes against the grain with Jack, who is a neat freak. Talk about opposites!

After a few minutes of small talk, Bill and his girlfriend depart for dinner. Jack completes his unpacking, thinking that Bill will return soon and they can get acquainted. At 11:30, Jack decides to get ready for bed because he is tired and has had a long day. He wants to be rested when orientation starts the next day. Exhausted from his trip and unpacking, Jack falls asleep very fast.

Suddenly, he hears loud voices coming down the hall. The voices belong to people who obviously have been drinking very heavily. The door to Jack's room opens and in walks Bill and his girlfriend. Bill turns on the light and continues to talk loudly and rudely. He and his girlfriend are having an argument. They act as though Jack is not even in the room. After a few angry exchanges, Bill shoves his girlfriend, who by now is crying and screaming profanities at him. She rushes from the room screaming at him. This certainly is not the roommate Jack has been hoping for. He is concerned that Mary will tolerate the abuse that Bill obviously takes for granted.

Bill bangs around the room for another 20 minutes before falling in bed. Within minutes, he is snoring loudly while Jack lies awake, unable to sleep. Finally, after two hours of tossing and turning, Jack falls asleep only to be awakened by the phone ringing incessantly. Bill continues to sleep because he has passed out from being so drunk. Jack drags himself out of bed and answers the phone. It's Bill's girlfriend, who is crying and asking to speak to Bill. Jack tells her that Bill is asleep and that she should call back the next day. He hangs up on her and gets back in bed. The phone continues to ring off and on for another hour. Jack never goes back to sleep.

Hardly able to get out of bed when the alarm goes off, Jack is very upset with his roommate, who is still snoring loudly. Thinking that Bill needs to go to orientation, Jack tries to wake him. He is rudely attacked with a string of vicious profanities. He takes his shower, dresses, and quietly exits the room.

When he returns after orientation around 2:00, thinking he might try to get some rest, he hears a girl giggling as he approaches the door to his room. When he walks in, he is stunned to find Bill and his girlfriend in bed—apparently, they have made up. He feels like an intruder in his own room. "Come on in. Don't mind us. You'll have to get used to Mary staying over. In fact, she'll probably spend every night here." Jack tells Bill that he has to leave for the bookstore. He is now really upset because he can't even go to his room and rest. He decides to talk to Bill when he returns, if Mary is gone.

Fortunately, Mary has gone back to her apartment, and this gives Jack a chance to talk. "Bill," he begins, "I've got a problem with the way things are going. First, you and Mary came in late last night and woke me up. Then you snored for the next 30 minutes, and then the phone rang all night. And you need to know that I don't approve of your having your girlfriend spend the night in our room. You don't have the right to just take over this room and ignore the fact that I live here too. I want to get along with you, but some things will have to change."

Bill is incensed. "Just my luck to get a prude like you for a roommate. I bet you don't even drink. Well, I didn't come to college to live like a priest, so you might as well get used to it because I'm going to do whatever I want to. I have waited for this day for a long time, and a little hick like you is not going to mess it up for me. And as for Mary, she will stay here anytime I want her to."

With those comments, Bill stomps out of the room. Jack is very depressed and distraught. He came to college to get an education, and there is no way this is going to work. Talking to Bill is like talking to a rock. "What do I do now? Clearly, this isn't going to work."

Case Study Analysis

Name _____ Date _____

Class _____ Section _____

1. What are the **facts** you KNOW about the case?

   _____
   _____
   _____

2. What are some **logical assumptions** you can make about the case?

   _____
   _____
   _____

3. What are the **problems** involved in the case as you see it?

   _____
   _____
   _____

4. What is the **root problem** (the main issue)?

   _____
   _____

5. What do you estimate is the **cause of the root problem**?

   _____
   _____

6. What are the **reasons** that the root problem exists?

   _____
   _____
   _____

7. What is (are) the **solution(s)** to the problem?

   _____
   _____
   _____

8. Are there any **moral and/or ethical considerations** to your solution?

_____

_____

_____

9. What are the **consequences** of your solution?

_____

_____

_____

10. What are the **"real-world" implications** for this case?

_____

_____

_____

11. How will the **lives** of the people in the case study **be changed** because of your proposed solution?

_____

_____

_____

12. Where are some **areas on campus** that one could get help with the problems associated with this case?

_____

_____

_____

13. Where are some **areas beyond the campus** that one could get help with the problems associated with this case?

_____

_____

_____

14. What **personal advice** would you give to Jack?

_____

_____

_____

Wellness

value, every letter, every Bible verse, and every lesson taught by her
parents and church will be challenged? Does Joy have the strength to
take this personal spiritual journey?

The absence of illness does not equal wellness. Wellness is as much mental,
emotional, and spiritual as it is physical. True wellness takes a commitment
much larger than people realize and takes years
to achieve and much willpower to maintain. From proper diet to spiritual issues
to challenging mental endeavors, wellness is a lifetime goal.

13

CASE 1 Heavy on My Mind

Agatha has always been a large woman. She has endured taunts and ridicule about her weight for years. She has convinced herself that college will be different. She believes that people are more mature in college and that her weight will not be an issue. Will the insensitive remarks of two classmates cost Agatha her college education?

CASE 2 The Great Balancing Act

Thomas is a nontraditional student who has returned to school years after having graduated from high school. When he graduated 10 years ago, he went into the Navy for 4 years. Today he is married, has two children, is working in a demanding job, and is going back to school. He realizes immediately that this is a balancing act that can produce great stress. Will he need a magician to help him with his new act?

CASE 3 Nobody Knows the Trouble I've Seen

Joy enrolls in a class called Faith, Doubt, and Reason, hoping to strengthen her spiritual wellness. Little does she know that every value, every tenet, every Bible verse, and every lesson taught by her parents and church will be challenged! Does Joy have the strength to take this personal spiritual journey?

Heavy on My Mind

Agatha makes it to class a few moments before the professor arrives. She takes her seat and can feel her heart racing and beating rapidly. She is out of breath and very tired from having walked the two blocks from her residence hall to the Academic Center. She always carries a washcloth in her purse so that she can wipe the sweat from her forehead throughout the day. She is panting heavily and sweating profusely as she scrambles to find her textbook, her notebook, and her pen. It is not a hot day; as a matter of fact, it is rather cool in the Northeast and many students are wearing sweaters. Agatha is not wearing a sweater; she is wearing a short-sleeve shirt and a skirt. Agatha is not a petite woman. She weighs nearly 250 pounds and has had a severe weight problem her entire life.

As she reaches for her textbook, her notebook falls to the floor and she can't reach it by leaning over. Reba, a student who sits beside Agatha, hands her the notebook and Agatha thanks her. Just as the professor is about to begin, Agatha hears two people behind her talking and one says, "Whew . . . that sure is a big girl there." The other student says, "Yeah, I'm glad I'm sitting over to the side and not behind her. I wouldn't be able to see the professor." They both laugh quietly. "Or the board," the other student says.

Agatha is hurt, but not overly upset, by the comment because today is no different for her than the past 19 years. She has heard all of the comments over the years. She has endured ridicule for her weight from her family, her doctors, and even her "friends." She knows every fat joke in the book and can pinpoint the scars on her soul left by vicious comments. Still, she is an upbeat, optimistic person. She is an A student and is attending Newton University on a full academic scholarship. "Some people have got the looks; I've got the brains," she tells herself and others.

After class, Reba strikes up a conversation with Agatha and the two agree to meet in the dining hall for supper at 6:00 P.M. Reba is impressed with Agatha's academic ability, having witnessed her answering almost every question in class today. Agatha is quite shy and is happy that a potential new friend has made the first effort. As the two women leave the class, Agatha hears a roaring laugh behind them. She has no idea who is laughing or what is so amusing. But in her mind, they are laughing at her walk, her size, her clothes, and her legs, which rub together because she is so large. "Just ignore them," she thinks to herself. "You've heard it all before."

At 6:00, Agatha and Reba meet outside the dining hall. As they eat dinner together, they realize just how much they have in common. Their musical tastes, love of theatre, and interest in

architecture are very similar. They discover that they both have an interest in becoming interior designers. By the end of dinner, they seem headed for a great relationship. They agree to meet the next afternoon for another dinner. Agatha is thrilled.

As the weeks progress, Agatha and Reba do become very good friends. They enjoy each other's company and have a wonderfully fun time when they are around each other. One day while waiting for class to begin, Agatha and Reba are talking when Reba takes a bag of raisins out of her purse. She leans across the isle and offers some to Agatha, who politely declines. At that moment, they both hear someone from the back of the room say in a loud voice, "Better watch it, you'll draw back a bloody stump offering food to her."

While Agatha knows the pain of ridicule, this statement is more than she can handle. She quickly gathers her books, rises from the desk, and walks briskly toward the door. As she reaches the door, she hears laughter, but she also hears Reba speaking in a very loud voice.

"You two have to be the most insensitive, ignorant, inhuman people at this university. Do you have no manners or feelings at all?" Reba yells as she gathers her belongings and heads for the door. "College is supposed to be a place where you grow up . . . so why don't you start today!!" she says as she exits the classroom.

"Agatha," Reba begins as she finds her at the end of the hallway. "They're just ignorant people who have no concern for human feelings. Don't let them get you down."

"I'll be OK," Agatha tells Reba. "It's just that I thought it would be different in college. I thought people would be more mature and care about more than looks and weight."

The two sit at the end of the hallway and talk for quite a while. Reba tries to comfort Agatha and help her concentrate on her positive qualities, her humor, and her superior academic standing. "You've got it all going for you," she tells Agatha. "Don't let two insensitive people hurt you."

"But you don't understand," Agatha pleads. "You're a small, pretty girl who doesn't have to worry about clothes or shoes or having people disregard you as worthless because you're fat. I mean totally negate you as a human being."

For the first time, Reba can read the pain in Agatha's face. She can see the damage from years of abuse and self-torture. "Agatha," Reba begins, "can I ask you something?"

"As long as it's not about Krispy Kreme," Agatha says as she wipes the tears from her eyes and tries to regain her composure through her usual humor.

"Have you ever seen a doctor about your weight issues?" Reba asks. "Now don't get mad or think that I'm trying to get in your business, but I've seen you eat many meals and you don't eat as much as I do. I've watched you at lunch and dinner, and I just don't get it."

"*You* don't get it," Agatha chuckles through the pain. "*I* don't get it either. I've tried every diet known to man. I've been on Weight Watchers, Jenny Craig, Atkins, Shakin' to the Oldies Program, the Cabbage Diet, the Fruit Diet, the yaddah, yaddah, yaddah diet. *Nothing* works. My doctor told me that I was not trying hard enough. He said that I needed to cut my food intake in half. So I tried that, and I was so hungry that I couldn't even function. He said that I needed to walk four miles a day. Reba, I can barely walk from my room to class. I'm just lost." Tears begin to form in Agatha's eyes again as she explains the turmoil of her life.

"What have other doctors said?" Reba asks.

"I've only been to my hometown doctor back in Greenville," Agatha replies.

"Do you want to look around for someone here?" Reba asks. "I'll help you, and we might find someone who knows more than your family doctor back home."

"I don't know," Agatha says. "I'm just so tired of it all. You'd think that being smart and kind and nice and helpful would be enough to get you through, but even here, that's not enough. It's all about how you look. I'm just tired."

Case Study Analysis

Name _____ Date _____

Class _____ Section _____

1. What are the **facts** you KNOW about the case?

   _____

   _____

2. What are some **logical assumptions** you can make about the case?

   _____

   _____

3. What are the **problems** involved in the case as you see it?

   _____

   _____

   _____

4. What is the **root problem** (the main issue)?

   _____

   _____

5. What do you estimate is the **cause of the root problem**?

   _____

   _____

6. What are the **reasons** that the root problem exists?

   _____

   _____

   _____

7. What is (are) the **solution(s)** to the problem?

   _____

   _____

   _____

8. Are there any **moral and/or ethical considerations** to your solution?

_____

_____

_____

9. What are the **consequences** of your solution?

_____

_____

_____

10. What are the **"real-world" implications** for this case?

_____

_____

_____

11. How will the **lives** of the people in the case study **be changed** because of your proposed solution?

_____

_____

_____

12. Where are some **areas on campus** that one could get help with the problems associated with this case?

_____

_____

_____

13. Where are some **areas beyond the campus** that one could get help with the problems associated with this case?

_____

_____

_____

14. What **personal advice** would you give to Agatha?

_____

_____

_____

The Great Balancing Act

Thomas McKissick has been out of school for 10 years. He spent 4 years in the Navy and has spent the last 6 years working as an airplane mechanic. Although he makes a good salary, he wants to get into management, and for this he must have a college degree. Thomas realizes that he will have a hectic schedule if he continues to handle all the responsibilities he has in his life, but he is determined to get this degree. He believes that it will mean a much better lifestyle for his family, and he is tired of his current job. Fortunately, the college he attends has accepted enough credits from his Navy courses to allow him to begin as a sophomore in engineering.

Thomas can't believe how difficult his Math course is. In high school, he had been a decent student and had never found Math that difficult, but he has apparently forgotten a great deal. He feels stressed out just thinking about it. Nor has English Literature been his favorite subject. He finds this course especially distasteful because the professor drones on and on in a monotone. He is tired when he gets to class, and this voice makes it difficult to listen. Further, the professor insists that they read a book a week along with the textbook. He is beginning to wonder if he can keep up in two courses and work and take care of his family.

When Thomas gets home after school that night, his wife, Deborah, tells him that his parents have called wanting him to do some yard work for them on the weekend. They are older and can't do their yard work anymore. Thomas has a brother who lives in the same city, but he never helps his parents, so all this falls on Thomas.

Thomas has gotten home too late to see his kids before they went to bed, and he feels badly about that because he leaves too early in the morning to spend much time with them. He also wonders when he and Deborah will ever have any time to be together. Deborah stays at home with the children, so she enjoys going out on weekends. His worries keep him awake until early in the morning, so he leaves for work very tired.

His new supervisor is a taskmaster and expects him and his colleagues to produce extraordinary amounts of work. Thomas takes his work very seriously because he knows lives depend on his being careful. This new boss doesn't seem to measure anything but how fast one gets a job done. He knows that the company's bottom line has been suffering due to the decrease in tourism and business travel. As a result, several employees in his department have been laid off, so he feels pressured to produce. His family certainly can't afford to have him lose his job. He tries to work faster and still be careful, and he can feel the tightness in his chest increasing as the day goes on. He is so anxious about his job that he takes only 20 minutes to eat his lunch quickly and get back to work.

Thomas rushes out of the building heading for class and hits the 5 o'clock traffic. As he inches along toward campus, he can feel his body getting tense and he curses as he tries to maneuver through traffic and get ahead. Finally, he gets to the parking lot, where it takes him 10 minutes to find a parking space. Running up the steps to class, he arrives 10 minutes late and faces the glaring eyes of his English professor. "Mr. McKissick, you cannot come to my class late and disturb everyone who is trying to learn. You will either have to get here on time or drop my class." Thomas wants to drop through the floor. By the time the class is over, he can hardly hold his head up because he lost so much sleep the night before. Driving home, he thinks about the Math homework that must be done by the next evening. "How will I ever get all this stuff done and spend any time with my family?" he wonders.

Thomas's schedule follows a similar pattern for the next three weeks. His mother calls needing more help; his own yard looks neglected; he misses his son's soccer game; and his boss yells at him at work. Deborah has been nice, but she obviously feels neglected. The kids clamor for his attention. It seems that everyone he knows wants a part of him. He is feeling so stressed that he is beginning to worry about his health if he keeps going at this pace.

That night, Deborah tells him that something has to give. She wants him to go to school, but this is having too much of a negative effect on their family life. His parents are driving her crazy calling all the time wanting Thomas to come and do things for them. Although he is working as fast as he can, his boss seems to think he is slacking off. To top it all off, he got a C– on his English paper.

Deborah tells him that Chip, their son, has been getting into trouble at school. Chip has never been a problem. The teacher, a male, feels that Chip is trying to get attention from him because he's not getting enough of his father's time. The pressure that has been building for a month suddenly explodes, and Thomas yells at Deborah. His yelling wakes Chip, who comes into the den crying, "I don't like my Daddy anymore. He's never home and when he is, he's mean to us." Thomas is devastated.

Case Study Analysis

Name _____ Date _____

Class _____ Section _____

1. What are the **facts** you KNOW about the case?

_____

_____

2. What are some **logical assumptions** you can make about the case?

_____

_____

_____

3. What are the **problems** involved in the case as you see it?

_____

_____

_____

4. What is the **root problem** (the main issue)?

_____

_____

5. What do you estimate is the **cause of the root problem**?

_____

_____

6. What are the **reasons** that the root problem exists?

_____

_____

_____

7. What is (are) the **solution(s)** to the problem?

_____

_____

_____

8. Are there any **moral and/or ethical considerations** to your solution?

_____

_____

9. What are the **consequences** of your solution?

_____

_____

10. What are the **"real-world" implications** for this case?

_____

_____

11. How will the **lives** of the people in the case study **be changed** because of your proposed solution?

_____

_____

12. Where are some **areas on campus** that one could get help with the problems associated with this case?

_____

_____

13. Where are some **areas beyond the campus** that one could get help with the problems associated with this case?

_____

_____

14. What **personal advice** would you give to Thomas?

_____

_____

CASE 3　Nobody Knows the Trouble I've Seen

Professor Elliott enters the classroom, greets the students, hands out a syllabus, calls the roll, and begins to speak about the class for which 30 students have registered. "This, as you know, is Religion 117, Faith, Doubt, and Reason," he begins. "We will be discussing the tenets of the Bible, Christianity in general, and faith in particular. I'll probably say things that will shock you and maybe even anger you, but this class is about testing the resolve of your faith and determining if you know enough about your proclaimed religion to take a stand. Are there any questions?"

The class is silent as Dr. Elliott waits for a response. "OK, then, we're off." He walks behind the desk, opens his briefcase, and takes out a book that is familiar to almost everyone in the room. He holds the book up in his left hand and asks, "Can anyone tell me what this book is?" Almost every hand in the class goes up. "You," he says to Aaron in the second row. "What is it?"

"It is the Holy Bible, sir."

"Ding, ding, ding," he mocks. "You're correct. Do you all agree?"

The students in the class all say yes as the book has "Bible" written across its front.

"Well, from this moment on, you can forget this crap!" he shouts as he throws the Bible into the air. He tosses the Bible like a Frisbee, and it hits the wall near the entrance door. The Bible lands near the metal trash can and comes to rest after sliding some five feet from Dr. Elliott. "That book was written by a bunch of crazy lunatics to make you give money to the church," he says sarcastically. "There was never a Jonah and the whale. There was never an Adam and Eve, and there was never any flood or famine. You're just fools for accepting what you've been told over the years. I plan to set you straight."

The students in the class, Aaron included, are in shock. They have never seen anyone throw a Bible onto the floor and call it crap. They have never heard anyone call the authors of the Bible "crazy lunatics," and they have certainly never heard anyone so rudely discuss other religions. The class sits painfully silent as they listen to his tirade.

When the next class period begins, Dr. Elliott enters and begins to pound away at almost every commonly held belief about the Bible. Finally, one student, Joy, raises her hand and says, "Dr. Elliott, I want you to know that I do believe in the Bible and I believe in God and I believe what my church has taught me."

"That's fine, Joy," Dr. Elliott says. "Does anyone else feel the way that Joy feels?"

Many students raise their hands and offer support to Joy.

"Well, Miss Joy," Dr. Elliott begins, "I'm going to ask that Donnovan right here, sitting in the front row, not sit there on Friday. Donnovan, I hope that is OK with you because Miss Joy is going to bring her God to class with her and we'll want him to sit up front. Is that OK with you, Miss Joy?" The class sits motionless. Dr. Elliott continues, "Why don't you bring your little God to class with you on Friday? If you believe in him so much and he's so powerful, why don't you just have him come and join us? He answers prayers, doesn't he? Well, you just pray that he shows up on Friday. Tell him we've got a seat for him." The class leaves numb.

Joy can't believe what has just transpired. She is literally in shock that a human being can be so cold and calculating *and* get paid for it. She decides that it is time to talk to her advisor and possibly drop the class. When she gets back to her room, she calls to make an immediate appointment. The meeting is scheduled for 4:00 that afternoon.

As Joy enters the advisor's office, she is nervous about discussing another professor's tactics with her. However, she does not know where else to turn. "Mrs. Gallows," Joy begins, "I have a real problem in my religion class." She continues until Mrs. Gallows is up to speed on the entire situation. "What should I do?" Joy asks.

"Well, Joy, this is a hard one. Let me tell you what I know about Dr. Elliott, and we'll see if this helps any. I have known him for over 15 years as a colleague, and I have to tell you that he is one of the nicest, most considerate faculty members at this college. I'm going to play the devil's advocate here and ask if you think you're overreacting, if you're too sensitive to the issue to see his real purpose, or if you seriously believe that he is damaging your religion? I know those are hard questions, but think about them for a moment."

"All I know is that he threw the Bible on the floor and called it crap and disputed almost every parable in the book," Joy says.

"Why did you take the class?" Mrs. Gallows asks.

"I took it so that I could understand more about my faith, my religion," Joy responds.

"So you took it to help with your spiritual wellness?" Mrs. Gallows questions.

"Well, I guess you could put it that way, although I've never thought about wellness in spiritual terms," Joy answers.

"You know that wellness is much more than being free of illness, Joy. It is about being well emotionally, physically, culturally, socially, and, yes, spiritually."

"Well, Dr. Elliott is certainly not helping me with my spiritual wellness. He has destroyed everything that I believe in. He has taken my faith and thrashed it on the floor and called it crap," Joy says almost tearfully.

"Can I ask you a personal question, Joy?" Mrs. Gallows says gently.

"Sure."

"Have you ever read the Bible?"

"Have I read the Bible?" Joy asks back almost angrily. "I go to church every Sunday, participate in Sunday School, and even teach Vacation Bible School in the summers," she replies.

"That is not what I asked you, Joy. Have you ever read the entire Bible from cover to cover, really looking at its contents, understanding its stories, dealing with its violence, grasping its true message? Have you ever spent a year with the Bible?"

Joy is embarrassed as she admits, "No, Mrs. Gallows, I have not read the whole Bible. But I have read most of it . . . . a lot of it."

"And you want to base your life's faith, your spiritual wellness, on a book of which you have only read parts?" Mrs. Gallows asks.

"No, I really don't, but I don't get the connection between my not having read the entire Bible and Dr. Elliott's blasting us for having a religion."

"Maybe he is just trying to get the entire class, regardless of faith, to look more closely at the teachings so that you can build your own spiritual path rather than accept the path that others gave you. Do you think that is a possibility?"

"I don't know," Joy replies. "Do you think I should drop the class until I figure this out?"

"Can you figure it out on your own?" Mrs. Gallows asks.

Case Study Analysis

Name _____ Date _____

Class _____ Section _____

1. What are the **facts** you KNOW about the case?
   _____
   _____
   _____

2. What are some **logical assumptions** you can make about the case?
   _____
   _____
   _____

3. What are the **problems** involved in the case as you see it?
   _____
   _____
   _____

4. What is the **root problem** (the main issue)?
   _____
   _____

5. What do you estimate is the **cause of the root problem?**
   _____
   _____

6. What are the **reasons** that the root problem exists?
   _____
   _____
   _____

7. What is (are) the **solution(s)** to the problem?
   _____
   _____
   _____

8. Are there any **moral and/or ethical considerations** to your solution?

_____

_____

_____

9. What are the **consequences** of your solution?

_____

_____

_____

10. What are the **"real-world" implications** for this case?

_____

_____

_____

11. How will the **lives** of the people in the case study **be changed** because of your proposed solution?

_____

_____

_____

12. Where are some **areas on campus** that one could get help with the problems associated with this case?

_____

_____

_____

13. Where are some **areas beyond the campus** that one could get help with the problems associated with this case?

_____

_____

_____

14. What **personal advice** would you give to Joy?

_____

_____

_____

Careers

AT A GLANCE

It is reported that most Americans fewer than 40 hours (an average workweek) deciding what they will do for 40 years. Few people know how to research a career, and fewer still have ever had a shadowing experience. In years past, people took jobs and kept those jobs for many, many years. Some stayed in their jobs their entire lives. Today, it is expected that you will not only change jobs frequently but that you will actually change careers three times during your working life.

CASE 1   When I Grow Up

The only thing Glynda has ever wanted to be is an elementary school teacher. Once enrolled in college, she immediately signs up to take an education practicum in the elementary school. Things do not go well at the beginning, but she has high hopes that they will improve. They do not. The situation goes from bad to worse, and she decides to drop the course and change her major. The biggest problem is that she does not have any idea of a future career. Will an apple a day do the trick?

CASE 2   Take Me to Your Leader

Koichi is one of those rare individuals who knows exactly what he wants to do when he gets out of college. He has never had any doubt about his career path. He will be the general manager of the most exclusive golf club in America! Part of his plan includes getting an early start in the industry through internships, shadowing, and mentoring. Will his age and cultural identity stand in his way?

CASE 3   Taking Care of Business

Megan leaves for a big university with "stars in her eyes" and plans to become an entrepreneur and own her own fashion design business. She soon learns that politics enters every situation and that change leaves no business untouched. Can she deal with the pressures of school and business colleagues?

When I Grow Up

Glynda's head hurts so badly at the end of the day that the only thing on which she can focus is getting home, taking aspirin, and going to bed . . . at 4:00 in the afternoon. "What have I gotten myself into?" she thinks as she makes her way to her car at the end of the day. "This is a complete disaster. Tomorrow has to be better," she silently prays. Tuesday is not any better, nor is Wednesday or Friday. Glynda leaves Johnson Middle School feeling like a complete failure. "And this is what I wanted to do for a living," she thinks.

"I've thought about teaching middle school for two years, and now that I'm doing my shadowing practicum, I hate it. I've made a huge mistake," she says to her friend Abby. "I don't like any part of it. The kids are disorderly, the room is overcrowded, the parents gripe at the smallest thing, and my supervising teacher just leaves me alone with them while she goes to the lounge. It's nothing like I thought it would be."

Glynda has entered Farmington College as an education major and has immediately registered for Education 110, Supervised Practicum. This course is designed to allow prospective teachers who are in their first or second semester of college to work in a school setting of their choice. This helps determine if they are suitable for the classroom—and if the classroom suits them. Her practicum professor, Dr. Mora, places Glynda at Johnson Middle School because she expresses a desire to teach seventh and eighth graders. When students are placed in the practicum, they are assigned a supervising teacher from the school. Dr. Mora does not know that Walker Hanson, Glynda's supervising teacher, leaves her alone with his class.

"Have you talked to Dr. Mora?" Abby asks. "Maybe he can help you. He needs to know that Hanson is leaving you alone with a class full of students."

"I don't want to complain," Glynda says. "That may make it worse. I think I'm just going to drop the class."

"Really?" Abby asks. "It's only been a couple of weeks."

"Let me tell you . . . that's enough," Glynda says. "If I never see that school, those kids, Hanson, or a blackboard again, it will be too soon."

"But if you drop the class, what are you gonna do?" Abby asks. "Do you think you'll take it again next semester?"

"After this, I don't think I want to be a teacher anymore," Glynda says.

Later in the week, Glynda goes to the records office and formally drops the Education 110. "Maybe now I'll be able to sleep and the headaches will stop," she thinks to herself.

On her way back to the residence hall, Glynda stops by the Dining Commons to grab a cup of coffee. She takes the coffee to the outside seating area and sits on a bench overlooking the campus's huge green lawn. Her mind is filled with thoughts of failure, thoughts of leaving school completely, and most frantically, thoughts of "what am I going to do now?" She is depressed and at a total loss about her future. "Teaching is all I planned for," she thinks to herself. "I've never considered another career. I just knew I'd love it."

As she sits there, she sees students walking past her carrying art port-folio bags or musical instruments, students wearing health care uniforms, students shooting a video on the grassy square, and students working with land survey equipment. "How do they know?" she thinks to herself. "How are they so happy with what they are doing?" Emotions overwhelm her. She is on the verge of tears but also angry at herself, Dr. Mora, and Mr. Hanson, and even jealous at those students walking past her, happy with their career decisions.

Glynda sits there for what seems like several hours, thinking about her practicum experience, reminiscing on the days in junior high and high school when she saw herself standing in front of eager students, teaching them about the world and places and people and survival and hope. "Hope," she thinks. "That's what I need some of now. I'm all out of hope."

As she stands to leave, Abby approaches her. "So what did you decide to do? Did you talk with Dr. Mora?"

"I dropped the class, Abby. I didn't know what else to do. My teaching career of three weeks is over," Glynda states sadly.

"I'm sorry that everything has played out this way," Abby says, trying to console her. "So what are you going to do now? What is the plan?"

"I plan to go to my room and have a nervous breakdown. That's my plan right now," she says as she tries to laugh the whole situation away.

As the following weeks pass, Glynda becomes more depressed than ever. She has trouble concentrating on her other classes because she does not see how they fit into her life anymore. "Children's Literature," she thinks. "What good is that now? When will I ever need Children's Literature?" Her mind is filled with irrational thoughts. "Without a major, I can't have a career. Without a career, I can't have a job. Without a job, I can't have friends because everyone will think I'm a lazy bum. Without friends, I'll never meet someone to love. Without someone to love, I'll never have children. Without children, why in the world would I ever need Children's Literature?"

Glynda is beyond consoling as Abby comes to her room to go to a movie as they had planned. "Are you ready to go?" Abby asks very happily. "The movie just got a rave review in the *Times* this morning. I can't wait."

"I'm not going," Glynda asserts.

"Not going?" Abby asks sharply. "Why not?"

"I don't feel like going out. I'm just going to stay here and watch TV," Glynda says.

"Oh yeah, that's really gonna help," Abby quips back sarcastically. "Maybe Monica or Phoebe or Chandler can help you."

"You don't understand," Glynda says in a pleading voice. "My dreams are gone."

"I understand that you seem to have given up. I understand that you seem to have lost your mind completely over one stupid course and one setback. That I understand," Abby says.

"But I wanted . . ." Glynda is interrupted by Abby.

"Yeah, you wanted to yaddah, yaddah, yaddah. You're 19 years old and are acting like a 90-year-old loser. I'm trying to help you, encourage you, and be your friend, but you're making it painfully difficult," Abby says. "You have got to get up out of that bed and find your way, girl, or you're gonna lose more than a career."

"What do you mean lose more . . . ?" She is interrupted again.

"Me," Abby says, "you're gonna lose me. I don't plan to stand by and watch you hang up your life and not even try to fix it, to not even try to find a way out. I thought you were stronger than this."

Case Study Analysis

Name _____ Date _____

Class _____ Section _____

1. What are the **facts** you KNOW about the case?

_____

_____

2. What are some **logical assumptions** you can make about the case?

_____

_____

_____

_____

3. What are the **problems** involved in the case as you see it?

_____

_____

_____

4. What is the **root problem** (the main issue)?

_____

_____

5. What do you estimate is the **cause of the root problem**?

_____

_____

_____

6. What are the **reasons** that the root problem exists?

_____

_____

_____

7. What is (are) the **solution(s)** to the problem?

_____

_____

_____

8. Are there any **moral and/or ethical considerations** to your solution?

9. What are the **consequences** of your solution?

10. What are the **"real-world" implications** for this case?

11. How will the **lives** of the people in the case study **be changed** because of your proposed solution?

12. Where are some **areas on campus** that one could get help with the problems associated with this case?

13. Where are some **areas beyond the campus** that one could get help with the problems associated with this case?

14. What **personal advice** would you give to Glynda?

Take Me to Your Leader

Koichi Iko is a fifth-generation Japanese-American whose family has been involved in banking for over 60 years. He has always known exactly what he would do with his life despite the fact that his grandfather and father want him to follow in their footsteps. They tell him frequently of the plans they have made for him and how easy it will be for him to take over their successful corporation. Koichi, or "Chi," as his friends call him, listens politely, but in his heart he knows this is not the way for him.

Chi enrolls in a large university in San Diego and selects Hospitality Management as his major with a specialization in Club Management. His plan is to do his graduate work at the University of South Carolina, which has a top-level Sports Business program as well as a Club Management specialization. The director of this program, Dr. Goodman, is known internationally as one of the best in her field. Chi's career track is laid out for him. Now, to implement all the facets of his dream.

Chi begins his semester with the typical freshman courses and one course in his field. He finds Introduction to Club Management so exciting. It is exactly what he has always wanted to do. Dr. Goodman is assigned as his advisor. This is a dream come true! How did he have such good fortune as to have this professor for whom he has so much admiration as his advisor? Dr. Goodman is encouraging and promises to help him find work in his field. She explains the program, including the fact that this degree requires both a practicum and an internship.

"The practicum," Dr. Goodman explains, "is completed between your freshman and sophomore years. University faculty do not supervise this internship; you do, however, have to write a detailed paper that covers all aspects of this work experience. Usually, you find this job on your own, but I know lots of people in the business, and I will help you if you need me to."

"The internship is completed between your junior and senior years. Occasionally, students complete it at the end of the senior year and take advantage of having completed more relevant course work. Then, if the internship works out well, you might stay with that club for your first real job." Dr. Goodman continues, "Most of our students do very well, Chi, and I am sure you will be no exception."

That night, Chi's father calls to talk about his experiences thus far. He is not happy when Chi tells him that he has selected the Hospitality major rather than Investment Banking. "I don't understand how you could give up such a wonderful opportunity that my father and I have worked so hard to give to you. You know, Koichi, I could insist that you major in banking. After all, I am paying the bills.

If you just knew how I struggled to pay my way through college, I am sure you would understand how I feel." Chi hates to disappoint his father and grandfather, but he knows in his heart that he will make them proud in the field he has chosen.

Chi knows from doing research that he needs to get work experience in his field. Although he has always worked, until this summer it has been in his family's investment banking firm. This past summer, he worked as a greens keeper for a public golf course in Los Angeles. This is a minor step toward his goal, but any experience usually helps. Chi knows that he needs more real, front-line experience in the hospitality and club management business.

He stops by Dr. Goodman's office that week and seeks her advice as to where he should start looking. She gives him several general managers' names, coaches him on what to expect, and tells him to let her know how things work out.

Excited to be looking for the first step in his career, Chi dresses in a navy suit. He looks immaculate as he walks in the front door of a very exclusive golf club. Mr. Warren comes out to meet him and takes him back to his office. Chi is very impressed with the exquisite office. The decor is decidedly upscale and features beautiful Oriental appointments. Through the floor-to-ceiling windows, he can see the beautiful golf club laid out behind him. This would be a perfect place for him to start his dream. "You know, Chi," Mr. Warren says, "we really don't need part-time employees right now, but Dr. Goodman has been my friend for a long time so I'm going to do her a favor. You need to know, however, that I will expect you to perform at the top-flight level. Anything less, and I won't be able to keep you around. Our membership is very selective."

Mr. Warren takes Chi around the club and shows him the dining room, the golf club, the pro shop, the pool area—all of which are lovely. He tells Chi that his first job will be working with Mrs. Channing, the director of catering. Mrs. Channing invites him to come by her office the next day ready for work. "I will give you an orientation program before you get started," she says. While Mr. Warren is there, she seems nice enough, but Chi senses that something is not quite right. He wonders what he's done to make her not like him.

Wanting to impress Mrs. Channing, Chi arrives early the next afternoon ready for work. "Well, I'm ready to learn, Mrs. Channing. Mr. Warren says you are excellent at your job and that I can learn a great deal from you." She mumbles a thank you and asks him to go with her to her office.

"Young man, someone needs to talk to you about this business. Obviously, you are nice enough and certainly you want to do well, but you are coming into this business with several strikes against you. Before you spend your entire college career preparing to be a general manager of a major club, you need to know the truth. It is virtually impossible for a Japanese-American to break into this business and work up to a general manager's position. These clubs are very exclusive, and their membership lists are private. They can be as discriminatory as they want to, and they will. I can take you and work with you in the catering department, and you might become a director of catering in a less exclusive club, but you will not become a general manager in a major private club. This may sound harsh, but I think you need to know the truth."

Chi is stunned and heartbroken. What should he say? His family is highly respected in Los Angeles by the Japanese-American community. Chi has never experienced this kind of treatment before. Could she be right? Or is this just the feeling of one prejudiced individual? Did his father know this? Is this the reason his father is so against his going into this field?

Case Study Analysis

Name _____ Date _____

Class _____ Section _____

1. What are the **facts** you KNOW about the case?
   _____
   _____
   _____
   _____

2. What are some **logical assumptions** you can make about the case?
   _____
   _____
   _____
   _____

3. What are the **problems** involved in the case as you see it?
   _____
   _____
   _____
   _____

4. What is the **root problem** (the main issue)?
   _____
   _____

5. What do you estimate is the **cause of the root problem**?
   _____
   _____

6. What are the **reasons** that the root problem exists?
   _____
   _____
   _____
   _____

7. What is (are) the **solution(s)** to the problem?
   _____
   _____
   _____

247

8. Are there any **moral and/or ethical considerations** to your solution?

_____

_____

_____

9. What are the **consequences** of your solution?

_____

_____

_____

10. What are the **"real-world" implications** for this case?

_____

_____

_____

11. How will the **lives** of the people in the case study **be changed** because of your proposed solution?

_____

_____

_____

12. Where are some **areas on campus** that one could get help with the problems associated with this case?

_____

_____

_____

13. Where are some **areas beyond the campus** that one could get help with the problems associated with this case?

_____

_____

_____

14. What **personal advice** would you give to Koichi?

_____

_____

_____

Taking Care of Business

Megan is a student at the University of Georgia, where she has chosen Business Administration as her major. Because her goal is to become an entrepreneur, she is very interested in her business courses. Since she was a little girl, she has dreamed of owning her own clothing design business. She is very excited to learn that a very successful designer, Christiaan Jacobs, has moved his business, Christiaan's Designs, from New York to Athens, Georgia, where she is going to school.

Megan makes an appointment with Mr. Jacobs and convinces him to give her a job in the afternoons so she can learn the design business from an expert. She can't believe her good fortune! What a great job for her resume when she is preparing to go out into the real world. And what a wonderful opportunity to learn and make spending money at the same time. Mr. Jacobs tells her that his company has been producing high-fashion clothes for over 12 years and that his line has been known for special touches that he has always incorporated into his designs. Megan wonders to herself if doing the same thing over and over in the fashion industry is a good thing, but what does she know? After all, she is here to learn from the best, so she dismisses her nagging thoughts.

At first, Megan is pretty much lost at work, but gradually she begins to catch on. Mrs. Reeves, an older woman who has worked with Mr. Jacobs for years, has taken her under her wing and is teaching her the business. Mrs. Reeves is a designer herself and created several very popular fashions several years ago.

Megan is very determined to break into this industry and is taking her business courses very seriously. She pores over her textbooks late into the night and is particularly interested in a chapter on "leading change." Her professor, Dr. Cannon, is a proponent of this theory: if it ain't broke, break it. Because Megan is captivated with his lectures, she looks for ways to implement Dr. Cannon's theories at work.

Megan often wonders about Mr. Cannon's "if it ain't broke" theory and decides that it must not apply to the fashion industry because most of the designs she sees appear to follow the "tried-and-true" pattern.

After Megan has been at Christiaan's Designs for about three weeks, Mr. Jacobs calls a meeting of all employees. His company employs over 200 people, and she is intrigued as she watches them file into the auditorium for this meeting. She sits by Mrs. Reeves, who is sharing with her ideas on what she might expect from this meeting. Mrs. Reeves notes that the group seems sparse and accounts for several people who are missing. She seems very curious about this meeting.

Mr. Jacobs wastes little time getting to his agenda. He begins by telling his employees that he has to share some bad news with them. The sales of Christiaan's Designs are declining dramatically. He tells the group that the company's designs have fallen out of favor with many of the Hollywood and television stars who made his creations so famous. Because of the downturn in business, he has had no choice but to implement major changes effective immediately. He tells the group that 75 of their fellow employees were given "pink slips" that afternoon and are cleaning out their work areas now and will be leaving the premises immediately. They will all be given a severance package that covers their salaries for one month. Mr. Jacobs goes on to tell the group how sorry he is but that it cannot be helped.

Megan hears Mrs. Reeves gasp at this terrible news. Mrs. Reeves cries silently at the thought of her beloved company in trouble and for her colleagues who are now without work.

Mr. Jacobs goes on to announce other changes. Effective immediately, his company is moving away from high-fashion couture and will begin designing for teenagers. His company has managed to secure a major contract for this line of clothes. His staff members are stunned. They have always designed high-fashion gowns for the rich and famous and cannot comprehend entering a mass market and having to vie for the attention of what they see as "fickle teens." Mr. Jacobs makes several other related announcements and then dismisses the meeting.

When she arrives at work the next afternoon, Megan is surprised to find the usually industrious Mrs. Reeves depressed. Still emotional, Mrs. Reeves confides in Megan that she just cannot bring herself to design clothes for teenagers after having been at the "top of her game." She blames Mr. Jacobs for the downturn in business and cites his "poor management skills." Megan overhears Mrs. Reeves talking to several colleagues during the afternoon and is surprised that she is trying to bring them into her camp of disgruntled workers. Rather than make any effort to adapt, Mrs. Reeves spends her time for the next several days in and out of colleagues' work areas, trying to stir them up against Mr. Jacobs. When Megan tries to encourage Mrs. Reeves, she is hostile to her and tells her she is too young and green to understand what is really going on. She tells Megan that she has submitted her resume to several other companies.

Megan also notes a number of people who appear to be "going through the motions" if any of the management team is on the floor but who quickly become lethargic and complaining when they leave. They don't seem to care if the business succeeds or not. Basically, they just want a paycheck. They join in with the other naysayers when no one is looking.

While Megan doesn't want to be disloyal to Mrs. Reeves, it has become obvious that she is not going to adapt to this change. Megan begins to observe the employees who appear to be willing and able to change their work styles and habits. Megan is confused about what her role should be and where she can go for advice.

The next day when she arrives at work, her supervisor, Mr. Tanner, drops by her workstation and asks her to come to his office, saying that he needs to talk to her. Megan is nervous and wonders what might be wrong. She questions why a manager would want to talk to her instead of a more senior person. When she is seated, Mr. Tanner asks her several very direct questions: "I see you talking to Mrs. Reeves. She seems unhappy. Do you know if she is?" "Do you know of others in the company who appear to be unhappy?" "Do you know if Mrs. Reeves is sending out her resume? Do you know to whom she is sending it?" "Can you give me the names of other people who may be planning to leave the company?"

Case Study Analysis

Name _____ Date _____

Class _____ Section _____

1. What are the **facts** you KNOW about the case?

   _____

   _____

2. What are some **logical assumptions** you can make about the case?

   _____

   _____

   _____

3. What are the **problems** involved in the case as you see it?

   _____

   _____

   _____

   _____

4. What is the **root problem** (the main issue)?

   _____

   _____

5. What do you estimate is the **cause of the root problem**?

   _____

   _____

6. What are the **reasons** that the root problem exists?

   _____

   _____

   _____

7. What is (are) the **solution(s)** to the problem?

   _____

   _____

   _____

8. Are there any **moral and/or ethical considerations** to your solution?

_____

_____

_____

9. What are the **consequences** of your solution?

_____

_____

_____

10. What are the **"real-world" implications** for this case?

_____

_____

_____

11. How will the **lives** of the people in the case study **be changed** because of your proposed solution?

_____

_____

_____

12. Where are some **areas on campus** that one could get help with the problems associated with this case?

_____

_____

_____

13. Where are some **areas beyond the campus** that one could get help with the problems associated with this case?

_____

_____

_____

14. What **personal advice** would you give to Megan?

_____

_____

_____

Glossary

Academic freedom   This is a term used by professors in institutions of higher education that allows them to conduct research and then be able to teach that research, regardless of controversial issues or subject matter. Academic freedom allows the professor the right to teach certain materials that might not have been allowed in high school.

Academic integrity   You have read, fully understand, and adhere to the policies, codes, and moral values of your institution. It implies that you will not cheat, plagiarize, or be unfair in your academic, social, cultural, or civic work.

Accreditation   Most high schools and colleges in the United States are accredited by a regional agency. This agency is responsible for insuring that a minimum set of standards are held at all institutions that are members in the accreditation agency. The Southern Association of Colleges and Schools is one example of an accreditation agency.

Adding   When a student adds a class during registration periods or during the first week of classes, it means that he will be taking an additional class in his schedule.

Administration   The administration of a college is usually made up of nonteaching personnel who handle all of the administrative aspects of the college. The administration is headed by the president and vice presidents. The structure of the administration at each college varies.

Advising   To make sure that you will know what classes to take and in which order, you will be assigned an academic advisor—most often a faculty member in your discipline or major—when you arrive on campus. This advisor will usually be with you during your entire degree. She is responsible for guiding you through your academic work at the college.

African-American studies   This curriculum deals with the major contributions by African-Americans in art, literature, history, medicine, sciences, and architecture. Many colleges offer majors and minors in African-American Studies.

AIDS This acronym stands for Acquired Immune Deficiency Syndrome, a disease that is transmitted sexually, intravenously, or from mother to child. Currently, no known cure for AIDS exists, but several medications, such as AZT and protease inhibitors, help to slow the deterioration of the immune system.

Alumna, Alumni, Alumnus These terms are used to describe students who hold degrees from a college. The term *alumna* refers to women, *alumni* refers to men, and *alumnus* refers to women and men. The term *alumni* is used most often.

Anti-Semitism Discrimination against people of Jewish or Arabic descent.

Articulation An articulation agreement is a signed document between two or more institutions guaranteeing that the courses taken at one college will transfer to another college. For example, if Oak College has an articulation agreement with Maple College, it means that the course work taken at Oak College will be accepted toward a degree at Maple College.

Associate degree The associate degree is a two-year degree that usually prepares the student to enter the workforce with a specific skill or trade. It is also offered to students as the first two years of their bachelor's, or four-year degree. Not all colleges offer the associate degree.

Attendance Each college has an attendance policy, such as "a student can miss no more than 10 percent of the total class hours or he will receive an F for the course." This policy is followed strictly by some professors and more leniently by others. You should always know the attendance policy of each professor with whom you are studying.

Auditing Most colleges offer the choice either to enroll in a course or to audit a course. If you enroll in a course, you pay the entire fee, attend classes, take exams, and receive credit. If you audit a course, the fee is usually lower, you do not take exams, and you do not receive credit. Course auditing is usually done by people who are having trouble in a subject or by those who want to gain more knowledge about a particular subject. Some colleges charge full price for auditing a course.

Baccalaureate The baccalaureate degree, more commonly called the bachelor's degree, is a four-year degree in a specific field. Although this degree can be completed in as few as three years or as many as six-plus years, traditionally the amount of academic work required is four years. This degree prepares students for such careers as teaching, social work, engineering, fine arts, and journalism, to name a few. Graduate work is also available in these fields.

Bankruptcy Bankruptcy is when a person must file legal papers through a lawyer to declare that she cannot pay her bills. Filing bankruptcy destroys one's credit history and it takes 10 years for the bankruptcy to disappear from one's credit report.

Binge drinking Binge drinking is defined as having five or more alcoholic beverages at one sitting.

Blackboard Blackboard is a delivery platform for distance education courses taken over the web. Several platforms exist, including WebCT and Course Compass.

Board of Trustees The Board of Trustees is the governing body of the college. The board is appointed by government officials (usually the governor) of each state. The board hires the president and must approve any curriculum changes to degree programs. The board also sets policy for the college.

Campus The campus is the physical plant of the university or college. The term refers to all buildings, fields, arenas, auditoriums, and other properties owned by the college.

Campus police Each college and university has a campus police office or a security office. You will need to locate this office once you arrive on campus so that, in case of emergency, you will be able to find it quickly. Campus security can assist you with problems ranging from physical danger to car trouble.

Carrel This is a booth or small room located in the library of the college. You can reserve a carrel for professional use throughout the semester or on a weekly basis. Many times, the carrel is large enough for only one person. Never leave any personal belongings or important academic materials in the carrel because they may be stolen.

Case study A case study is a story based on real-life events. Cases are written with open-ended conclusions and somewhat vague details to allow the reader to critically examine the story and develop logical solutions to resolve issues.

Catalog The college catalog is a book issued to you at the beginning of your college career. This book is one of the most important tools that you will use in developing your schedule and completing your degree. The catalog is a legally binding document stating what your degree requirements are for the duration of your study. You will need to obtain and keep the catalog of the year in which you entered college.

Certificate A certificate program is a series of courses, usually one year in length, designed to educate and train an individual in a certain area, such as welding, automotive repair, medical transcription, tool and die, early childhood, physical therapy assistance, and fashion merchandising. While these programs are certified and detailed, they are not degrees.

Often, associate and bachelor's degrees are offered in these areas as well.

CLEP The College Level Examination Program, or CLEP, is designed to allow students to "test" out of a course. CLEP exams are nationally normalized and often are more extensive than a course in the same area. If you CLEP a course, it means that you do not have to take the course in which you passed the CLEP exam. Some colleges have limits on the number of hours that can be earned by CLEP.

Club drugs Club drugs are drugs taken at raves, parties, or dance clubs. Some of the most common club drugs are GHB (gamma hydroxybutyrate), ecstasy, roofies, and meth.

Cognate A cognate is a course (or set of courses) taken outside of your major. Some colleges call this a minor. For instance, if you are majoring in English, you may wish to take a cognate in History or Drama. Cognates are usually chosen in a field close to the major. It would be unlikely for a student to major in English and take a cognate in Pharmacy.

Communications College curricula often state that a student must have nine hours of communications. This most commonly refers to English and Speech (oral communication) courses. The mixture of these courses will usually be English 101 and 102 and Speech 101. This will vary from college to college.

Comprehensive exams This term refers to exams that encompass materials from the entire course. If you are taking a History course and your instructor informs you that there will be a comprehensive exam, information from the first lecture through the last lecture will be included on the exam.

Continuing education Almost every college in the nation offers courses in continuing education or community education. These courses are not offered for college credit, but Continuing Education Units are awarded in many cases. These courses are usually designed to meet the needs of specific businesses and industries or to provide courses of interest to the community. Continuing education courses range from small engine repair to flower arranging, from stained glass making to small business management.

Co-op This term is used to refer to a relationship between business/industry and the educational institution. During a co-op, the student spends a semester in college and the next semester on the job. Some co-ops may be structured differently, but the general idea behind a co-op is to gain on-the-job experience while still in college.

Cooperative learning In cooperative learning, learning, exploration, discovery, and results take place in a well-structured group. Cooperative learning teams are groups that work together on research, test preparation, project completion, and many other tasks.

Corequisite A corequisite is a course that must be taken at the same time as another course. Many times, science courses carry a corequisite. If you are taking Biology 101, the lab course Biology 101L may be required as the corequisite.

Counseling Most colleges have a counseling center on campus. Do not confuse counseling with advising. Trained counselors assist you with problems that might arise in your personal life, with your study skills, and with your career aspirations. Academic advisors are responsible for your academic progress. Some colleges do combine the two, but in many instances, the counselor and the advisor are two different people with two different job descriptions.

Course title Every course offered at a college will have a course title. You may see something in your schedule of classes that reads: ENG 101, SPC 205, HIS 210, and so forth. Your college catalog will define what the abbreviations mean. ENG 101 usually stands for English 101, SPC could be the heading for speech, and HIS could mean history. Headings and course titles vary from college to college.

Credit Credit is money or goods given to you on a reasonable amount of trust that you can and will repay the money or pay for the goods. Credit can come in several forms; credit cards and loans are the most common. Credit can be very dangerous to a person's future if he has too much credit or does not repay the credit in time.

Credit hour A credit hour is the amount of credit offered for each class that you take. Usually, each class is worth three credit hours. Science courses, foreign languages, and some math courses are worth four credit hours because of required labs. If a class carries three credit hours, this usually means that the class meets for three hours per week. This formula may vary greatly in a summer session or midsession.

Credit score Your credit score is calculated by the amount of debt you have, your salary, your payment history, your length of residence in one place, and the number of inquiries into your credit history, to name a few. Your credit score is used to determine if you will be extended future credit and the interest rate that you will be charged. A low score could mean that you cannot get credit or that you will pay a very high interest rate. Negative credit reports stay on your credit history for seven years.

Critical thinking Critical thinking is thinking that is purposeful, reasoned, and goal directed. It is a type of thinking used to solve problems, make associations, connect relationships, formulate inferences, make decisions, and detect faulty arguments and persuasion.

Curriculum The curriculum is the area of study in which you are engaged. It is a set of classes that you must take in order for a degree to be awarded.

Dean   The word *dean* is not a name, but a title. A dean is usually the head of a division or area of study. Some colleges might have a Dean of Arts and Sciences, a Dean of Business, and a Dean of Mathematics. The dean is the policy maker and usually the business manager and final decision maker of an area of study. Deans usually report to vice presidents or provosts.

Dean's list   The dean's list is a listing of students who have achieved at least a 3.5 (B+) on a 4.0 scale (these numbers are defined under GPA). This achievement may vary from college to college, but generally speaking, the dean's list consists of students in the top 5 percent of students in that college.

Default   A default is when a person fails to repay a loan according to the terms provided in the original loan papers. A default on a Guaranteed Student Loan will result in the garnishment of wages and the inability to acquire a position with the government. Also, you will receive no federal or state income tax returns until the loan is repaid. Further, a Guaranteed Student Loan cannot be written off under bankruptcy laws.

Degree   When a student completes an approved course of study, she is awarded a degree. The title of the degree depends on the college, the number of credit hours in the program, and the field of study. A 2-year degree is called an associate degree, and a 4-year degree is called a bachelor's degree. If a student attends graduate school, she may receive a master's degree (approximately 2 to 3 years) and sometimes a doctorate degree (anywhere from 3 to 10 years). Some colleges even offer postdoctorate degrees.

Diploma   A diploma is awarded when an approved course of study is completed. The diploma is not as detailed or comprehensive as

an associate degree and usually consists of only 8 to 12 courses specific to a certain field.

Distance learning   Distance learning is learning that takes place away from the campus. Distance learning or distance education is usually offered by a computerized platform such as Blackboard, WebCT, or Course Compass. Chat sessions and Internet assignments are common in distance learning.

Dropping   When a student decides that he does not enjoy a class or will not be able to pass the class because of grades or absenteeism, he may elect to drop that class section. This means that the class will no longer appear on his schedule or be calculated in his GPA. Rules and regulations on dropping vary from college to college. All rules should be explained in the catalog.

Ecstasy   Ecstasy, or "X," is a "club drug" that is very common at raves and dance parties. It produces a relaxed, euphoric state, which makes the user experience warmth, heightened emotions, and self-acceptance. It can cause severe depression and even death among some users. X is illegal to use or possess.

Elective   An elective is a course that a student chooses to take outside of her major field of study. It could be in an area of interest or an area that complements the chosen major. For example, an English major might choose an elective in the field of theatre or history because these fields complement each other. However, a student majoring in English might also elect to take a course in medical terminology because she is interested in that area.

Emeriti   This Latin term is assigned to retired personnel of the college who have performed exemplary duties during their professional careers. For example, a college president who obtained new buildings, added curriculum programs, and increased the endowment might be named President Emeriti upon his or her retirement.

Ethnocentrism Ethnocentrism is the practice of thinking that one's ethnic group is superior to others.

Evening college The evening college program is designed to allow students who have full-time jobs to obtain a college degree by enrolling in classes that meet in the evening. Some colleges offer an entire degree program in the evening; others offer only some courses in the evening.

Faculty The faculty of a college is the body of professionals who teach, do research, and perform community service. Faculty members have prepared for many years to hold the responsibilities carried by this title. Many have been to school for 20 or more years to obtain the knowledge and skill necessary to train students in specific fields.

Fallacy A fallacy is a false notion. It is a statement based on false materials, invalid inferences, or incorrect reasoning.

Fees Fees refer to the amount of money charged by a college for specific items and services. Some fees may include tuition, meal plans, books, and health and activity fees. Fees vary from college to college and are usually printed in the catalog.

Financial aid If a student is awarded money from the college, the state, the federal government, private sources, or places of employment, this is referred to as financial aid. Financial aid can be awarded on the basis of either need or merit or both. Any grant, loan, or scholarship is formally called financial aid.

Fine Arts Many people tend to think of Fine Arts as drawing or painting, but in actuality, the Fine Arts encompass a variety of artistic forms. Theatre, dance, architecture, drawing, painting, sculpture, and music are considered part of the Fine Arts. Some colleges also include literature in this category.

Foreign language Almost every college offers at least one course in foreign languages. Many colleges offer degrees in this area. For schools in America, foreign languages consist of Spanish, French, Russian, Latin, German, Portuguese, Swahili, Arabic, Japanese, Chinese, and Korean, to name a few.

Fraternities A fraternity is an organization of the Greek system in which a male student is a member. Many fraternities have their own housing complexes on campus. Induction for each is different. Honorary fraternities, such as Phi Kappa Phi, also exist. These are academic in nature and are open to males and females.

Freshman This is a term used by high schools and colleges. The term *first-year student* is also used. This term refers to a student in his first year of college. Traditionally, a freshman is someone who has not yet completed 30 semester hours of college-level work.

GHB, or gamma hydroxybutyrate GHB is a club drug that comes most often in an odorless, liquid form but can also come as a powdery substance. At lower doses, GHB has a euphoric effect and can make the user feel relaxed, happy, and sociable. Higher doses can lead to dizziness, sleepiness, vomiting, spasms, and loss of consciousness. GHB and alcohol used together can be deadly.

GPA, or grade point average The grade point average is the numerical grading system used by almost every college in the nation. GPAs determine if a student is eligible for continued enrollment, financial aid, or honors. Most colleges operate under a 4.0 system. This means that all A's earned are worth 4 quality points; B's, 3 points; C's, 2 points; D's, 1 point; and F's, 0 points. To calculate a GPA, multiply the number of quality points by the number of credit hours carried by the course and then divide by the total number of hours carried. For example: If a student is taking English 101, Speech 101, History 201, and Psychology 101, these courses usually carry 3 credit hours each. If a student made all A's, she would have a GPA of 4.0. If the student made all B's, she would have a 3.0. However, if she had a variety of grades, the GPA would be calculated as follows:

	Grade	Credit	Q.Points	Total Points
ENG 101	A	3 hours x	4 =	12 points
SPC 101	C	3 hours x	2 =	6 points
HIS 201	B	3 hours x	3 =	9 points
PSY 101	D	3 hours x	1 =	3 points

30 points divided by 12 hours would equal a GPA of 2.5 (or C+ average)

Grace period   A grace period is usually 10 days after the due date of a loan payment. For example: If your car payment is due on the first of the month, many companies will give you a 10-day grace period (until the 11th) to pay the bill before they report your delinquent payment to a credit scoring company.

Graduate teaching assistant You may encounter a "teaching assistant" as a freshman or sophomore. In some larger colleges and universities, students working toward master's and doctorate degrees teach undergraduate, lower-level classes under the direction of a major professor in the department.

Grant   A grant is usually money that goes toward tuition and books that does not have to be repaid. Grants are most often awarded by state and federal governments.

Hepatitis   Hepatitis has three forms: A, B, and C. Hepatitis A comes from drinking contaminated water. Hepatitis B is more prevalent than HIV and can be transmitted sexually, through unsterile needles, and through unsterile tattoo equipment. Left untreated, hepatitis B can cause serious liver damage. Hepatitis C develops into a chronic condition in over 85 percent of the people who have it. Hepatitis C is the leading cause of liver transplants. Hepatitis B and C can be transmitted by sharing toothbrushes, nail clippers, or any item contaminated with blood. Hepatitis B and C have no recognizable signs or symptoms. Some people, however, do get flu-like symptoms, loss of appetite, nausea, vomiting, or fever.

Higher education   This term is used to describe any level of education beyond high school. All colleges are called institutions of higher education.

Homophobia   Homophobia is the fear of homosexuals or homosexuality.

Honor code   Many colleges operate under an honor code. This system demands that students perform all work without cheating, plagiarism, or any other dishonest actions. In many cases, a student can be removed from the institution for breaking the honor code. In other cases, if students do not turn in fellow students who they know have broken the code, they, too, can be removed from the institution.

Honors   Academic honors are based on the GPA of a student. Each college usually has many academic honors, including the dean's list, the president's list, and departmental honors. The three highest honors awarded are Summa Cum Laude, Magna Cum Laude, and Cum Laude. These are awarded at graduation for students who have maintained a GPA of 3.5 or better. The GPA requirement for these honors varies from college to college. Usually, they are awarded as follows:

3.5 to 3.7 Cum Laude

3.7 to 3.9 Magna Cum Laude

4.0 Summa Cum Laude

Honors college The honors college is usually a degree or a set of classes offered for students who performed exceptionally well in high school.

Humanities The Humanities are sometimes as misunderstood as the Fine Arts. Courses in the Humanities include History, Philosophy, Religion, and Cultural Studies; some colleges also include Literature, Government, and Foreign Languages. The college catalog will define what your college has designated as Humanities.

Identification cards Identification cards are essential for any college student. Some colleges issue them free, while some charge a small fee. The ID card allows the student to use the college library, participate in activities, use physical fitness facilities, and many times attend college events for free. They also come in handy in the community. Movie theatres, museums, zoos, and other cultural events usually charge less or nothing if a student has an ID. The card will also allow the student to use most area library facilities with special privileges. ID cards are usually validated each semester.

Identity theft Identity theft is when another person assumes your identity and uses your credit, your name, and your social security number. Identity theft can't always be prevented, but to reduce the risk, always guard your credit cards, your address history, and most important, your social security number and your driver's license number.

Independent study Many colleges offer courses through independent study, meaning that no formal classes and no classroom teacher are involved. The student works independently to complete the course under the general guidelines of a department and with the assistance of an instructor. Many colleges require that a student maintain a minimum GPA before enrolling in independent study classes.

Internship An internship involves working in a business or industry to gain experience in one's field of interest. Many colleges require internships for graduation.

Journal Many classes, such as English, freshman orientation, Literature, History, and Psychology, require students to keep a journal of thoughts, opinions, research, and class discussions. Many times, the journal is a communication link between the students and their professors.

Junior This term refers to a student who is enrolled in his third year of college or a student who has completed at least 60 credit hours of study.

Late fee A late fee is an "administrative" charge that lenders assess if a loan payment is late.

Learning style A learning style is the way an individual learns best. Three learning styles exist: visual, auditory, and tactile. Visual means that one learns best by seeing, auditory means that one learns best by hearing, and tactile means that one learns best by touching.

Lecture A lecture is the "lesson" given by an instructor in a class. The term usually refers to the style in which material is presented. Some instructors have group discussions, peer tutoring, or multimedia presentations. The lecture format means that the professor presents most of the information.

Liberal arts The liberal arts consist of a series of courses that go beyond training for a certain vocation or occupation. For instance, a student at a liberal arts college might be majoring in Biology, but he will also have to take courses in Fine Arts, History, Social Sciences, Math, "hard" sciences, and other related courses. The liberal arts curriculum insures that the student has been exposed to a variety of information and cultural experiences.

Load   A load refers to the amount of credit or the number of classes that a student is taking. The normal "load" for a student is between 15 and 18 hours, or five to six classes. For most colleges, 12 hours is considered a full-time load, but a student can take up to 18 or 21 hours for the same amount of tuition.

Major   A major is the intended field of study for a student. The major simply refers to the amount of work completed in one field; in other words, the majority of courses have been in one related field, such as English, Engineering, Medicine, Nursing, Art, History, or Political Science. A student is usually required to declare a major by the end of the sophomore (or second) year.

Meal plan   A meal plan is usually bought at the beginning of the semester and allows a student to eat a variety of meals by using a computer card or punch system. Meal plans can be purchased for three meals a day, breakfast only, lunch only, or any combination of meals.

Mentor   A mentor is someone whom a student can call on to help her through troubled times, assist her in decision making, and give advice. Mentors can be teachers, staff members, fellow outstanding classmates, or higher-level students. Mentors seldom volunteer to be a mentor; they usually fall into the role of mentoring because they are easy to talk with, knowledgeable about the college and the community, and willing to lend a helping hand. A student may, however, be assigned a mentor when she arrives on campus.

Methamphetamine   Crystal meth, as it is commonly called, is an illegal drug sold in pills, capsules, powder, or rock forms. It stimulates the central nervous system and breaks down the user's inhibitions. It can cause memory loss, aggression, violence, and psychotic behavior.

Minor   The minor of a student is the set of courses that he takes that usually complements the major. The minor commonly consists of six to eight courses in a specific field. If a student is majoring in Engineering, he might minor in Math or Electronics, something that would assist him in the workplace.

Multiple intelligence   Multiple intelligence is one of eight intelligences with which we are born. Howard Gardner, who believes that we all have one of eight intelligences as our primary strength, introduced the theory. The intelligences include Music/Rhythm, Logic/Math, Visual/Spatial, Naturalistic, Interpersonal, Intrapersonal, Verbal/Linguistic, and Body/Kinesthetic.

Natural and Physical Sciences   The Natural and Physical Sciences refer to a select group of courses from Biology, Chemistry, Physical Science, Physics, Anatomy, Zoology, Botany, Geology, Genetics, Microbiology, Physiology, and Astronomy.

Networking   Networking refers to meeting people who can help you (or whom you can help) find careers, meet other people, make connections, and "get ahead."

Online classes   Used in conjunction with distance learning or distance education, online classes use the Internet as a means of delivery, instead of a traditional classroom.

Orientation   Every student is requested, and many are required, to attend an orientation session. This is one of the most important steps that a student can take when beginning college. Important information and details concerning individual colleges and their rules and regulations will be discussed.

Plagiarism   This term refers to the act of using someone's words or works as your own without citing the original author. Penalties for plagiarism vary from college to college, but most institutions have strict guidelines for dealing with students who plagiarize. Some institutions force the student to withdraw from the institution. Your student handbook should list the penalties for plagiarism.

Prefix A prefix is a code used by the Office of the Registrar to designate a certain area of study. The prefix for English is usually ENG; for Religion, REL; for Theatre, THE; for History, HIS; and so forth. Prefix lettering varies from college to college.

Preprofessional programs Preprofessional programs usually refer to majors that require advanced study to the master's or doctoral level to be able to practice in the field. Such programs include, but are not limited to, Law, Medicine, Dentistry, Psychiatry, Nursing, Veterinary Studies, and Theology.

Prerequisite A prerequisite is a course that must be taken before another course. For example, most colleges require that English 101 and 102 (Composition I and II) be completed before any Literature course is taken. Therefore, English 101 and 102 are prerequisites to Literature. Prerequisites are always spelled out in the college catalog.

President A college president is the visionary leader of an institution. She is usually hired by the Board of Trustees of a college. Her primary responsibilities involve financial planning, fundraising, community relations, and the academic integrity of the curriculum. Every employee at the college is responsible to the president.

Probation Many times, a student who has below a 2.0 in any given semester or quarter will be placed on academic probation for one semester. If that student continues to perform below 2.0, suspension may be in order. The rules for probation and suspension must be displayed in the college catalog.

Professor Many people believe that all teachers on the college level are professors. This is not true. A full professor is someone who may have been in the profession for a long time and someone who usually holds a doctoral degree. The system of promotion among college teachers is as follows:

> adjunct instructor
> instructor
> lecturer
> assistant professor
> associate professor
> full professor (professor).

Protease inhibitors Protease inhibitors are a series, or "cocktail," of drugs used to fight HIV/AIDS and slow the destruction of the immune system. They have been instrumental in extending the lives of people living with HIV and AIDS. However, a new strain of HIV has arisen that is immune to the protease inhibitors presently used.

Provost The provost is the primary policy maker at the college with regard to academic standards. He usually reports directly to the president. Many colleges will not have a provost but will have a vice president for academic affairs or a dean of instruction.

Racism Racism occurs when a person or group of people believes that their race is superior to another race.

Readmit When a student has "stopped-out" for a semester or two, he will usually have to be readmitted to the college. This term does not apply to a student who elects not to attend summer sessions. Usually, no application fee is required for a readmit student. He does not lose his previously earned academic credit unless that credit carries a time limit. For example, some courses in Psychology carry a 5- or 10-year limit, meaning that if a degree is not awarded within that time, the course must be retaken.

Registrar The registrar has one of the most difficult jobs on any college campus. She is responsible for all student academic records. The registrar is also responsible for entering all grades and all drops and adds, printing the schedule, and verifying all candidates for graduation. The Office of the Registrar is sometimes referred to as the Records Office.

Residence hall A residence hall is a single-sex or co-educational facility on campus where students live. Many new students choose to live on campus because residence halls are conveniently located. They are also a good way to meet new friends and become involved in extracurricular activities. The college usually provides a full-time supervisor for each hall and a director of student housing. Each hall usually elects a student representative to be on the student council.

Residency requirement Many colleges have a residency requirement, meaning that a certain number of hours must be earned at the "home" institution. For many two-year colleges, at least 50 percent of the credit used for graduation must be earned at the home college. For four-year colleges, many requirements state that the last 30 hours must be earned at the home college. All residence requirements are spelled out in the college catalog.

Room and board If a student is going to live on campus, many times the fee charged for this service will be called "room and board." This basically means a place to stay and food to eat. Many students may opt to buy a meal plan along with their dorm room. These issues are usually discussed during orientation.

Root problem The root problem is the main issue, the core of the situation at hand. Most troublesome situations have several problems, but usually one major "root" problem exists that causes all of the other problems.

Scholar A scholar is usually someone who has performed exceptionally in a certain field of study.

Section code At many larger colleges, many sections of the same course are offered. The section code tells the computer and the registrar which hour and instructor the student will be in a particular class. A typical schedule may look something like this:

English 101 01 MWF 8:00–8:50 Smith
English 101 02 MWF 8:00–8:50 Jones
English 101 03 T TH 8:00–9:15 McGee

The numbers 01, 02, and 03 refer to the section of English in which the student wishes to enroll.

Senior The term *senior* is used for students in their last year of study for a bachelor's degree. The student must have completed at least 90 credit hours to be a senior.

Sexism Sexism is discrimination based on sex and social roles.

Sexual harassment Sexual harassment is defined as any type of advance that is unwanted by the receiver, including touching another person, taunting a person verbally, denying promotions based on forced relationships, and so forth.

Social Sciences The Social Sciences are courses that involve the study or interface with society and people. Social Science courses may include, but are not limited to, Psychology, Sociology, Anthropology, Political Science, Geography, Economics, and International Studies.

Sophomore The term *sophomore* refers to students who are in their second year of study for a bachelor's degree. A student must have completed at least 30 credit hours to be a sophomore.

Sororities Sororities are organizations of the Greek system in which females are members.

Many sororities have on-campus housing complexes. Initiation into a sorority differs from organization to organization and campus to campus.

Staff Personnel in the college setting are usually divided into three categories: administration, staff, and faculty. The staff is responsible for the day-to-day workings of the college. Usually people in admissions, financial aid, the bookstore, housing, student activities and personnel, and so forth hold staff titles. The people heading these departments are usually in administration.

Student Government Association (SGA) This is one of the most powerful and visible organizations on the college campus. Usually, the SGA comprises students from each of the four undergraduate classes. Annual elections are held to appoint officers. As the "student voice" on campus, the SGA represents the entire student body before the college administration.

Student loan Unlike a grant, a student loan must be repaid. The loans are usually at a much lower rate of interest than a bank loan. For most student loans, the payment schedule does not begin until six months after graduation. This allows the graduate to find a job and become secure in her chosen profession. If a student decides to return to school, she can get the loan deferred, with additional interest, until she completes a graduate degree.

Suspension Suspension may occur for a variety of reasons, but most institutions suspend students for academic reasons. While GPA requirements vary from college to college, usually a student is suspended when his grade point average falls below a 1.5 for two consecutive semesters. The college catalog contains the rules regarding suspension.

Syllabus In high school, you may have been given a class outline, but in college, you are given a syllabus. This is a legally binding contract between the student and the professor. This document contains the attendance policy, the grading scale, the required text, the professor's office hours and phone number(s), and important information regarding the course. Most professors also include the class operational calendar as a part of the syllabus. This is one of the most important documents that you will be issued in a class. You should take it to class with you daily and keep it at least until the semester is over.

Tenure You may hear someone call a college teacher a "tenured professor." This means that the professor has usually been with the college for many years and has been awarded tenure due to her successful efforts in research, publication of books and articles, and community service. Usually, tenure insures the professor lifelong employment.

TOEFL TOEFL is an acronym for the Test of English as a Foreign Language. This test is used to certify that international students have the English skills needed to succeed at the institution or to become a teaching assistant. Some colleges allow international students to use TOEFL to satisfy English as their foreign language requirement.

Tolerance Tolerance is the ability to recognize and respect the opinions, practices, religions, race, sex, sexual orientation, ethnicity, and age of other people.

Transcript A transcript is a formal record of all work attempted and completed at a college. If a student attends more than one college, he will have a transcript for each college. Many colleges have a policy in which all classes, completed or not, remain on the transcript. Some colleges allow D's and F's to be removed if the student repeats the course with a better grade. Many colleges, however, leave the old grade and continue to count the D or F in the

GPA. Rules regarding transcripts vary from college to college. Many employers now require that a prospective employee furnish a transcript from college.

Transfer This term may refer to course work or to a student. If a student enrolls in one college and then wants to go to another, she is classified as a transfer student. The course work completed is called *transfer work*. Many colleges have rules regarding the number of credit hours that may be transferred from one college to another. Most colleges will not accept credit from another college if the grade on the course in below a C.

Transient A transient student is someone who is attending another college to take one or two courses. If a student comes home for the summer and wants to enroll in a college near his home and maintain himself as a student at his chosen college, he is a transient student.

Transitional studies Many colleges have an open admission policy, meaning that the door is open to any student. In these cases, the college usually runs a transitional studies program to assist the student in reaching her educational goal. If a student has not performed well in English, Math, or Reading, she may be required to attend a transitional studies class to upgrade basic skills in certain areas.

Veterans Affairs Many colleges have an Office of Veterans Affairs to assist those students who have served in the military. Many times, a college will accept credit earned by a veteran while in the service. Most of the time, a veteran's financial package will differ because of the GI Bill.

Vice president Many colleges have several vice presidents who serve under the president. They are senior-level administrators who assist with the daily operations of the college. Most colleges have vice presidents of academic affairs, financial affairs, and student affairs, to name a few.

Volumes This term is used by most libraries in the nation. A volume is a book or a piece of nonprinted material used to assist the student in his studies. You may read that a college library has 70,000 volumes. This means that it has 70,000 books and other pieces of media. Many colleges have volumes that range in the millions.

WebCT WebCT is a delivery platform for distance education courses taken over the web.

Who's Who This is a shortened title for *Who's Who in American Colleges and Universities*, a nationally recognized grouping. Students are nominated by the college because of their academic standing and their achievements in cocurricular activities and community service.

Women's Studies Some colleges offer majors and minors in Women's Studies. The curriculum is centered around the major contributions of women to art, literature, medicine, history, law, architecture, and sciences.